PREACHING ESSENTIALS

A PRACTICAL GUIDE

Lenny Luchetti

wesleyan
publishing
house

Indianapolis, Indiana

Copyright © 2012 by Lenny Luchetti
Published by Wesleyan Publishing House
Indianapolis, Indiana 46250
Printed in the United States of America
ISBN: 978-0-89827-558-2

Library of Congress Cataloging-in-Publication Data

Luchetti, Lenny.
  Preaching essentials : a practical guide / Lenny Luchetti.
    p. cm.
  ISBN 978-0-89827-558-2
  1. Preaching. I. Title.
  BV4211.3.L83 2012
  251--dc23
                                        2011051977

To the churches and students who have found the grace
not only to learn from me, but also to teach me so much
about Christ and proclaiming him to the world.

To Amy, Zach, Lia, and Sam, who patiently loved me even
when the laptop computer seemed to be my all-consuming focus.

To the God who used preaching and preachers to reorient
my life toward him, and then called me to preach.

CONTENTS

Part 3. Preparation and Presentation

Part 4. Planning and Progress

Part 5. Postscript

ACKNOWLEDGEMENTS

I remember writing one of my first major papers in college. The research and writing took many hours. Because getting a good grade on this paper was important to me, I gave it to one of my more intelligent friends to proofread. I reassured him, "This is good stuff." He laughed his way through the entire paper and then asked me, "Len, are you really going to give this to your professor?"

When I sent the proposal for this book along with a few chapters to Keith Drury, Wayne Schmidt, and Harry F. Wood, and inquired, "Do you think there's a need for a book like this on preaching?" they responded with enthusiastic support. They didn't laugh at me, but pushed me to "go for it." These three wise men have served as my ministry mentors through writings, observations, and conversations, so I heeded their words. If they, like my college buddy, would have laughed at my work, I might not have had the moxie to submit the proposal.

Keith Drury is especially worthy of my thanks. He read the entire manuscript and gave me insightful feedback that, no doubt, made this book better than it would have been.

I am grateful to the team at Wesleyan Publishing House—Don Cady, Craig Bubeck, and Kevin Scott—whose excitement for the book and optimism concerning its potential heightened my own excitement and optimism.

My colleagues at Wesley Seminary make the vocation of teaching so much fun. We eat, think, debate, teach, and pray together. Their energetic love for Christ, the church, and students inspired me to write a book like this one.

Amy, my wife, always believed that I would finish the book and, once I did, that it would be worth reading, even when I doubted both. She is a rock indeed!

God amazes me. He used something as odd as preaching to initiate the reorienting of my life toward him. As if that wasn't enough, he even called me to preach so that through my voice, he might do for others what he did for me. Just when I thought it couldn't get any better, God led me into the vocation of helping other preachers "find their voice." I thank God in advance if you discover or recover your God-given voice for preaching by reading this book.

Lenny Luchetti

May 2012

INTRODUCTION

Reading this book reveals two things about you. First, it evidences your commitment to learn how to preach or how to preach better. Second, it demonstrates you are crazy or, to put it more mildly, daring enough to believe that the God of the universe might show up through the preacher's sacrament of words to transform people to transform the world. You are committed and courageous. A fruitful preaching life is impossible without this crucial combination of characteristics.

There are no shortcuts to good preaching, because good preaching requires good preachers. It takes God some time to form good preachers. This book is designed to foster the skills and habits necessary for the development and delivery of quality sermons. But God is the only one who can develop and deliver good preachers. Simply put, unless the Lord builds the preacher, preaching is in vain. My prayer is that this book will lead to good preaching convictions and practices that align with what God is already up to in forming good preachers.

Preaching Essentials: A Practical Guide is written for both new and seasoned preachers. New preachers will discover some of the important issues in preaching today, along with the skills needed to tackle the homiletic craft. Seasoned preachers will find reminders of what they may have forgotten, reinforcement to support their recent homiletic hunches, and renewal for their preaching soul. This book is also written to assist people like me who teach homiletics to new and seasoned preachers.

The reader is more than welcome to skip around in the book, but the chapters are ordered to mirror the rhythm of the preaching life and the homiletics course. In part 1, Preaching and Preachers, we explore some of the healthy foundations, convictions, and habits that prepare the preacher for the nuts and bolts of preaching. Part 2, People and Places, invites preachers to reflect on how our perspective on the particular people to whom we preach influences how and what we preach. The largest and most practical portion of the book is part 3, Preparation and Presentation. This section, as its name implies, moves the reader through the steps involved in the process of preparing and presenting sermons. Part 4, Planning and Progress, provides tools for the development of both the annual preaching calendar and the preacher. In part 5, Postscript, the reader will find some miscellaneous but critical afterthoughts that didn't seem to fit tightly in any other section.

Preaching Essentials: A Practical Guide is, I hope, neither theologically shallow nor homiletically simplistic. It is, however, intentionally designed to be accessible, readable, and practical to as many preachers as possible across the gamut of experience, education, ecclesiology, and ethnicity. The book is written to be *accessible* to all preachers no matter where they find themselves in their homiletic journey. The format of the contents and the brevity of the chapters make the book *readable*. The exercises at the end of every chapter help the book maintain its *practical* orientation.

Going up the mountain to encounter God through the biblical text in order to come down into the preaching event with something life-giving for God's people is quite an adventurous vocation. Can there be anything more exhilarating, frightening, and risky than the practice of preaching? If preaching merely required the acquisition of rhetorical skills, it would be less risky, for sure, but not nearly as thrilling. Rhetorical skills are helpful, but preaching depends on so much more. Effective preaching relies heavily upon the preacher's relationships with God, the biblical text, and the listeners. The preacher who cultivates the capacity to love all three is likely to preach in a manner that is faithful, fruitful, and fulfilling.

PART 1

PREACHING AND PREACHERS

1

WHY KEEP PREACHING?

Some scholars and preachers are suggesting that preaching has run its course. They say the craft served its purpose back when we were a word-based culture, but today a monologue seems like an outdated mode of communication. The proclamation of words from one talking head to a nodding (or sleeping!) crowd for twenty to thirty minutes, or worse, forty to fifty minutes, is a bygone byproduct of a different era when words mattered. Today, we are an image-based culture. The plethora of words we encounter every day, online or in print, has caused words to become meaningless. Music and other art forms have greater potential to impact people than the traditional sermon. And why should the pastor be *the* authority on matters of biblical interpretation? Dependence on the preacher was appropriate back when many people were uneducated and illiterate. Today, however, biblical resources abound and are accessible to most everyone. Why limit ourselves by listening to only one voice week after week when there is a multiplicity of voices in the church? Simply put, preaching is a useless and therefore unnecessary tool for the development of disciples. An Internet blogger named Kevin says it all when he writes, "We have hardly had any preaching at Grace Church for the last three years—haven't missed it!"

Why would anyone keep preaching in a twenty-first-century American context that seems to value preaching less today than ever? While I believe preaching must change in substantial ways, here are a few reasons why I keep on preaching and encourage you to do the same.

PREACHING IS BIBLICAL

According to the biblical story, words matter. God did his best work through words. Through words God formed the world and everything in it. For centuries, the Old Testament prophets communicated messages from God to his people essentially through words. The primary ministry of Jesus and John the Baptist was preaching (Mark 1:4, 38; Luke 8:1). Jesus recruited the apostles to preach (Mark 3:14; Luke 9:2), and the first-century church, according to the book of Acts, focused significant attention on the ministry of proclaiming good news. According to the Bible, words about, from, and for God proclaimed to a group of people through an anointed person will always be meaningful, relevant, and powerful even when considered passé. That is why we preach.

PREACHING IS A PORTAL FOR GOD

Will Willimon, seasoned pastor and prolific author, reminds us of the impossibility of preaching: "Getting up to preach was like trying to put out a thousand acre forest fire with a garden hose."[1] Thanks Willimon! Preaching is crazy. Arranging choice words in the right order because of a call from God, knowing full well that those words are dead bones unless God speaks through them, is utterly ridiculous. While we study and work diligently in our homiletic craft, we recognize that the power of preaching is more dependent on God showing up than the preacher.

Ironically, the ridiculous nature of preaching may be the very rationale in support of its ongoing practice in the life of the church. The practice of preaching repeatedly reminds us that God can and does accomplish the impossible through impossible methods. He just might decide to show up through the so-so words of a so-so preacher and transform so-so people into disciples who change the world! It makes sense that God might do this through music, a dramatic sketch, or an inspiring piece of art. It doesn't make much sense that God would use something as common as words to come to us, but he does. Just like he comes to us through the common bread and wine of Communion, so God comes to us through common words strung together by some common being we call preacher. That is why we preach.

PREACHING SETS PEOPLE FREE

The preaching of Martin Luther King, Jr., enabled African-Americans to reimagine themselves as people set free by Jesus Christ. Because of that reimagining, an oppressed group sought the liberation that they, through Christ, believed they already possessed. The act of preaching, words woven together to passionately proclaim the gospel, started the civil rights ball rolling with so much momentum that nothing but God could stop it. And why would he, since he is the one who got that ball rolling in the first place?

Preaching inspires middle-aged women and men to leave lucrative careers and go to the most frightening places in the world to build schools, hospitals, and orphanages. Preaching does that! Preaching rescues couples whose marriages are hanging by a thread so that instead of calling it quits they hold on "for better or worse" and begin to thrive. Preaching does that! Preaching brings hope to a lonely and lifeless teenager so that she resists the temptation to commit suicide. Preaching does that! Preaching causes a high school dropout alcoholic to believe that God just might use him as a pastor. Preaching does that! Maybe we haven't seen as much liberation as we long to see, but perhaps we've seen enough to convince us that preaching still has the power to bring freedom to the prisoner and recovery of sight to the blind, to set captives free by proclaiming the year of the Lord's favor (see Luke 4:14–21).

PREACHING PURIFIES THE PREACHER

The practice of preparing and presenting sermons on a regular basis has done wonders for my soul. God used the practice of preaching to breathe the winds of hope back into the deflated sails of my life on many occasions. The act of preaching has given me the audacity to believe what I am tempted to stop believing about God, myself, and the world. Preaching helps me to imagine a whole new world that is more real than the "virtual reality" within which I am sometimes compelled to live. The practice of preaching brings me deeper into the church, invites me to give sacrificially to the church, and prevents me from giving up on the "earthen vessel" known as the church. The call to preach pushes me toward purity and away from self-centered narcissism. I'm still not "all that," but you should have seen my life before the practice of preaching laid its hands on me!

PREACHING MATTERS

I know I'm preaching to the choir. Perhaps you don't need to be convinced that every moment you spend preparing to deliver your sacrament of words, as heart-wrenching and nerve-racking as it is, will be well worth the blood, sweat, and tears you pour into the homiletic task. But I need convincing at times. Does preaching still matter? If you're a preacher, you better believe it!

EXERCISES

1. Consider which one of the reasons for the ongoing practice of preaching listed above is most compelling to you and why.

2. Add some other reasons to the list in support of the ongoing practice of preaching in the life of the local church.

3. Reflect on how preaching has changed your life. What impact has the practice of preaching had on or through you?

NOTE

1. Steve Brown, Haddon Robinson, and Will Willimon, *A Voice in the Wilderness: Clear Preaching in a Complicated World* (Sisters, Ore.: Multnomah, 1993), 15–16.

2

YOU KNOW YOU'RE CALLED TO PREACH IF . . .

Determining whether or not God is calling you to pastoral ministry is hard enough, but discerning a call to the specific ministry of preaching is extremely challenging. The call from God to preach is, in most cases, an invitation enveloped in mystery. Is there a way for people to know intuitively, if not definitively, whether they are called to preach? I think so.

Albert Outler, Wesleyan historian and theologian, observed that John Wesley developed his theology and processed ministry decisions through four lenses: Scripture, tradition, reason, and experience. Outler labeled this grid the "Wesleyan Quadrilateral."

SCRIPTURE

What role has God's Word played in your contemplation of the call to preach? Are there key Bible passages that deeply resonate with you, pointing you toward the call? One of the Bible passages that impacted my call to preach is Leviticus 26:13, which reads, "I am the LORD your God, who brought you out of Egypt so that you would no longer be slaves to the Egyptians; I broke the bars of your yoke and enabled you to walk with heads held high." Through this verse, God was cultivating in me a passionate desire to partner with him in breaking the bars and lifting the heads of the human race through the power of Christian preaching.

TRADITION

How does your Christian tradition (in other words, your local church or denomination) view the call to preach and the role preaching plays within the life of a congregation? Do the leaders of your local church and denomination sense and support your call to preach? My call to preach was sparked and confirmed through the pastor and people of my local church. They affirmed my gifts and asked me questions that initiated my wrestling with the call to preach. Are there people with the gift of wisdom and discernment in your Christian community who see in you the potential and passion to preach the gospel?

REASON

A divine call inviting a human to speak words that describe the will and way of God is too odd to be reasonable. It does seem sensible, however, for the potentially called person to reflect on how their natural abilities and acquired skills might reinforce the call to preach. What abilities and skills make your call, or potential call, seem reasonable? Remember, of course, that God often does what seems unreasonable to us.

EXPERIENCE

What experiences in your life have shaped you for preaching the gospel? What challenges, disappointments, failures, accomplishments, and relationships have you encountered that led you toward the call to preach? One of the life experiences that shaped my call to preach was not being raised in the church. The experience of being an unchurched, nominally religious person heightens my ability to connect with the same kind of people through my preaching. What life experiences point you toward and prepare you for the call to preach?

CONVICTION

On several occasions, due to apparent failure, fatigue, or frustration, I have wanted to quit preaching. The conviction I am called by God to preach is often the one thing, the only thing, that gives me the audacity to keep opening my mouth, hoping the Holy Spirit will fill it with words worth speaking. Confidence in the call from God to preach not only gives the preacher the audacity, but the anointing, authority, and authenticity so desperately needed for preaching today.

EXERCISES

1. All Christians have a testimony, but those called to preach also have a "call-imony." Spend a few minutes reflecting on your call to preach and write your call-imony using the outline of Scripture, tradition, reason, and experience.

2. If you are still trying to discern whether or not you are called to preach, consult God. Prayerfully articulate to God, perhaps by journaling your thoughts, where you are in the journey of discernment. Then, listen for any impressions God might give you from Scripture, tradition, reason, and experience.

3. Consult a mentor or two who can help you explore the call to preach. Schedule some time with a preacher you respect or a layperson with the gift of wisdom. Share some notes from your call-imony and invite them to speak into your life regarding the vocation of preaching.

3

THEOLOGY MATTERS

Theology is impractical, irrelevant, and inaccessible to regular people with real problems who live in the real world."

"Studying the doctrine of the incarnation is not going to help me pay my bills and overcome my addictions."

"An exploration of how the divine persons within the Trinity relate to each other can't possibly help me with my marriage and parenting."

My ears have heard and, admittedly, my mouth has voiced statements like the ones above. Sometimes preachers even boast about how we avoid theology in order to proclaim "relevant messages that really connect." The assumption is that theological doctrines, such as the incarnation and the Trinity, are less relevant and therefore less important than the concerns that surface in the "real world."

The reflective preacher realizes, however, that theology (words about God) will always be relevant. Doctrines remind us who God is and teach us how to be relevant to him. The doctrine of Christ's incarnation reminds us that God has already made himself relevant to us and has paved a way for us to be relevant to him. The doctrine of the Trinity reminds us that God is fundamentally relational. Therefore, the way we humans are privileged to know and experience the Godhead three in one is through loving relationships with him and each other. Could there be anything more relevant to our lives than this?

One of my convictions is that the sermon, while it must certainly intersect with the needs and struggles of the human race, should ultimately reveal God. If it does not, then the preacher simply becomes a therapist or self-help guru instead of a pastoral theologian who proclaims the triune God and the incarnate Christ to a hope-needy human race.

There are two habits that can assist the preacher in developing and delivering sermons that proclaim the eternally relevant God. These habits involve asking theological questions and reading theological works. Here are six theological questions that impact preaching, followed by six recommended theological books.

SIX THEOLOGICAL QUESTIONS FOR PREACHERS

1. What does the overall story of the Bible reveal about the nature of God?

2. How does this sermon faithfully reflect what the biblical story overall reveals about God?

3. What does God seem to be saying and doing in and through this particular biblical text?

4. How does the purpose of the sermon align with the purposes of God manifest in this text?

5. What does the sermon say about the Father, the Son, and the Holy Spirit that is true, insightful, and compelling?

6. Does the sermon present the gospel by both honestly assessing the problem of human sin and hopefully proclaiming the resolution of divine grace?

SIX THEOLOGICAL BOOKS FOR PREACHERS

Most of the following theological resources can be accessed for free on the Internet. As you read these works, try to reflect on them in light of the ministry of preaching. Additionally, recognize that all of the theologians below hashed out their theology not in some academic ivory tower but in the context of pastoral ministry.

1. *On the Incarnation* by Athanasius (fourth century): This work will compel the preacher to ponder both the deity and humanity of Jesus Christ. The primary question the preacher will wrestle with while reading this work is, "Who is Jesus?" The follow-up question is, "How can my preaching incarnate the Son of God incarnate?"

2. *On Christian Doctrine* by Augustine of Hippo (late fourth to early fifth century): Book IV of this important work deals specifically with "The Christian Orator." As you read this section of the ancient book, you may be surprised by its contemporary import.

3. *Summa Theologiae* by Thomas Aquinas (thirteenth century): You may not want to read this massive work in its entirety, but there are several sections in the *Summa* ("summary") that are well worth the preacher's time, including "Treatise on Gratuitous Graces."

4. *Institutes of the Christian Religion* by John Calvin (sixteenth century): Like the *Summa*, this is an exhaustive theological work. The preacher will want to take in book 4, chapter 3, which is focused on "teachers and ministers."

5. *A Plain Account of Christian Perfection* by John Wesley (eighteenth century): Don't let the title scare you away from this important read. Wesley described perfection as intensity of love

for God and love for people. The preacher who embodies these two loves will proclaim the gospel with great impact.

6. *Church Dogmatics* by Karl Barth (twentieth century): Barth is not the easiest theologian to grasp, but chapter IV, "The Proclamation of the Church," is a gem worth reading and rereading. This chapter will, at the very least, guide preachers in considering the role of God in the preaching event.

CONCLUSION

Theological wisdom can and should shape the mind and heart of the pastor for preaching. When we interact with a diversity of theological voices within the church that span centuries and perspectives, our thoughts about God expand and appreciate for our particular theological tradition increases. Asking theological questions and reading theological classics cultivates not only better preaching but, more importantly, better preachers.

EXERCISES

1. As you prepare your next sermon, reflect on the six theological questions above and respond to each with a few sentences. Over time, the practice of theologically reflecting on your sermon will become an instinctive habit.

2. Read one of the theologians above every two weeks until you have read them all. As you read, be on the lookout for preaching wisdom from these thoughtful pastoral theologians.

4

SCIENCE OR ART?

The post-Enlightenment era of modernity upheld scientifically empirical data as the highest form of knowledge. The thinking went as follows: The most accurate information we humans can acquire is validated through scientific experimentation. This epistemological presupposition found its way through the cornfields of biblical scholarship and into the nearby field of homiletics. For several centuries now, many sermons have sounded much like logical arguments designed to *prove* the sermon's thesis. There may be a place for sermons like these from time to time, but the modernistic veneration of empirical proof has monopolized the preaching scene in a manner that causes the science of preaching to suffocate the art of preaching. While science is, by and large, designed to inform, art is uniquely designed to inspire. In the post-Christian, information-overloaded context within which most churches and preachers live, information without inspiration is impotent. Simply put, it is time for preachers to recover the art of preaching, without neglecting some of the science that guides our work.

FORMULAIC TO ORGANIC

Like many preachers over the past few centuries, I used to think of sermon development and delivery as pure science, kind of like chemistry. So I would mix an exact amount of exegetical study with at least three illustrations, one of them humorous, throwing in three possible sermon applications and *voilà*—out comes the sermon. Effective preaching today, however, seems to be artistically organic, not scientifically contrived or maneuvered. Preaching a sermon is like painting a landscape through which people glimpse God and his kingdom, and actually begin to see themselves in that kingdom landscape. The preacher-artist looks for creative ways to inspire the specific people within a given preaching context. In a sense, then, the sermon is an organically homegrown art form. There are, to be sure, scientific rules that govern every art form, like how to mix various shades to form a specific color. However, art that is truly art is not stifled by rules.

OBJECTIVE DETACHMENT TO
RELATIONAL INTIMACY

Scientific exploration necessitates the detached objectivity of the explorer toward the object. It is no wonder, then, that when preaching becomes a science that neglects the art of the craft, it comes across to listeners as stale, passionless, and distant. Good art, to the contrary, requires intimacy between the artist (the preacher) and the subjects (God, Scripture, and people). Preaching primarily as a science demands that the preacher divorce personality, relationship with listeners, and intimacy with God from the homiletic process. Art, on the other hand, requires intimacy. The best musicians, painters, and poets cannot detach themselves from their work; the art flows out from some place deep within them. Preaching as an art form entails preaching from the deepest places of the soul to the deepest needs of the human race. There is no way a preacher can do this kind of soul preaching as a detached, objective, and mechanical discipline. Something powerful happens when the Spirit of God, the Word of God, and the people of God mix, like colors of paint, with the soul of the preacher.

CONCLUSION

If preachers are going to paint a compelling picture of Christ and what it looks like to live in relationship with him, the preacher must throw him- or herself completely into the text of Scripture and the task of preaching. Preachers who go at their work like scientists, maintaining detached objectivity, will find that their sermons fall short of inspiring people to live into the redemptive reality called the kingdom of God.

EXERCISES

1. Reflect on your present sermon preparation process. What steps in your development of the sermon are more of a science and which are more of an art?

2. Preaching as an art form requires that the preacher move beyond objective detachment in order to deeply connect with God, the biblical text, and the congregation. What exercises can you include in your sermon preparation process to facilitate preaching as an art form?

5

PITFALLS TO AVOID

Getting off to a good start in the ministry of preaching is important. There are a few pitfalls that most new preachers encounter and from which some never fully recover. Knowing the mistakes to avoid is really half the battle. The other half is working hard to evade them. This chapter is simply a heads-up for new preachers and a reminder for seasoned ones. The following five pitfalls are dangerous but avoidable.

DIVORCING

Too many preachers have been taught to divorce the devotional reading of Scripture from the exegetical study of Scripture. The wrong-headed assumption is that the preacher who explores the biblical text in a devotional manner will ignore the exegetical dynamics (in other words, the historical background and word meanings) in the text. Isn't it possible, and even advisable, for the preacher to both prayerfully and critically engage the biblical text? While it is important to explore the biblical text based on the historical and literary contexts surrounding the text, can't the preacher simultaneously wrestle in a devotional manner with what God might be saying through the text to the preacher and the congregation?

In chapter 16, I focus on how to critically engage the biblical text on its terms. In chapter 17, I suggest some practical ways for preachers to explore a biblical text devotionally throughout the homiletic process. The preacher must avoid a divorce between the devotional and exegetical reading of Scripture. When the biblical text penetrates the life of the preacher, the sermon flowing out of that text is more likely to penetrate the hearts of listeners.

OVERLOADING

Many preachers spend between ten and fifteen hours each week studying a biblical text and developing the sermon. If the preacher shared every exegetical insight discovered during study and all of the illustrations that fit with those insights, the sermon could last for two hours! I remember one of my earliest sermons called "6 Godly Traits Found in Joseph," which covered chapters 37 to 50 in Genesis. It took me nearly an hour to preach this sermon, which was essentially six sermons rolled into one. Sometimes we preachers are tempted to include in the sermon every thought or idea that we conceive, even if they don't reinforce the focus of the sermon. Overloading the sermon with exegetical rabbit trails, unnecessary technical details, and a plethora of anecdotal illustrations prevents the sermon from reaching the homiletic pot of gold called clarity. See chapter 18 for guidance on how to bring more focus to the sermon.

HOPPING

Pastors get upset when congregants engage in what some call "church hopping." These hoppers go to your church one week, then another church the next week, and still a third church the following week. Pastors try to muster up the nerve to tell them, in love, of course, "Find one church and commit to it; stop church hopping." One of the pitfalls we preachers fall into if we're not careful is text hopping. Text hopping is when we hop around in the Bible from text to text to text while preaching our sermons. Some lay people may wish to tell their preacher, "Find one text of Scripture and commit to it; stop text hopping." Of course, the topical sermon by its nature invites multiple voices from Scripture to weigh in on the topic. Even still, the topical sermon must attend to those texts without quickly proof-texting and hopping to the next text. People come away from the text-hopping sermon with many good Bible verses, but ones that may not really reinforce the main focus of the sermon.

I used to think that what made a sermon biblical was the amount of Scripture I used in the sermon. Today, I am convinced that what makes a sermon biblical is its ability to say and do what God, through the biblical text, seems to be saying and doing. "Biblical," then, has nothing to do with the amount of Scripture but instead one's approach to Scripture. Being a mile wide and an inch deep is OK for a topical Bible study; but a sermon, in most cases, should find one main theme and drill down deep or the people to whom we preach might come away dazed and confused. If the sermon is going to strike deep into the hearts of listeners, it must drill down deep into a biblical passage to identify a primary focus that is faithful to the text and the congregational context.

SLOPPING

I used to think that if I had tasty and fresh ingredients in my sermon, such as powerful illustrations, challenging applications, and insightful exegetical nuggets, then it didn't make a difference how those ingredients were brought together. I threw all of the ingredients into the sermon without much thought to the order in which they were added. The sermon was like a brownie mix. The brownie recipe doesn't require any sequencing of ingredients; you just throw the powdered mix, eggs, water, and oil together into the bowl in no particular order and everything turns out OK. But there are some recipes that require you to add ingredients in the proper order or you will ruin the food. My wife and I bake bread in one of those bread-making machines. Our favorite recipe requires that water, sugar, and yeast are added first. Then, after about ten minutes in the machine, the oil, flour, and salt are supposed to be added. We discovered the hard way that ignoring the sequencing of ingredients can be disastrous.

The sermon is less like the brownie recipe and more like the bread recipe. Once the preacher has all of the elements that will be included in the sermon, careful and prayerful thought should guide how those elements are ordered within the sermon structure. Avoid slopping the parts together thoughtlessly, as I had a habit of doing for the first few years of my ministry. Consider the best time to add each ingredient to the sermonic recipe.

RANTING

Let's be honest, most of us preachers like to talk more than most people are willing to listen. If this is true, perhaps we should assist our listeners by talking less. Every context has its own standards regarding sermon length (see chapter 13), but regardless of context, most listeners are opposed to the ranting of their preacher. There are several forms of homiletic ranting, but most can be categorized as pet peeves or habitual redundancy.

All preachers have a few pet peeves that, if unchecked, keep surfacing in our sermons and utterly exasperate listeners. I know of one preacher who included in every sermon, no matter the text or topic, his diatribe about the evils of psychology. Some preachers avoid the diatribe but are guilty of careless repetition. Strategic repetition can be a powerful tool for sermonic clarity, as we consider in chapter 19. But when the sermon goes an extra fifteen minutes because the preacher simply, and not so creatively, repeats the same thing three times, it drives listeners toward the border of frustration.

The pitfall of ranting can be remedied. First, develop a preaching plan that incorporates a well-balanced diet of Scripture and topics (see chapter 32). Second, try writing out your next sermon word for word. This exercise can alleviate the tendency in preachers to rant and rave. Finally, don't feel guilty for preaching a sermon that is forty-five instead of sixty minutes or thirty instead of forty-five minutes. Less is more when it comes to preaching today. Reduce your sermon length by cutting out the soap-box rants and unnecessary repetition. God will, I promise, still love you even if you reduce the length of your sermons. And, your congregation will love you even more for developing tighter, more precise sermons that do not waste their time with redundant ranting.

EXERCISES

1. As you reflect on these five pitfalls, which two do you intuitively evade and which two do you need to intentionally avoid?

2. Explain and discuss these five pitfalls with your church staff, board, or a few trusted laypeople. Ask them to honestly respond to

the following questions: Which of the five pitfalls do you think I
tend to avoid? Which of the five pitfalls must I learn to avoid? The
level of honesty and transparency needed for this exercise is obviously high. Choose people who love you and the church enough to
tell you the truth concerning the strengths and areas for your
improvement in preaching.

6

HEALTHY PREACHERS S.H.E.D.

The preacher who develops a healthy plan to S.H.E.D. the superhero, messiah complex that leads to stress and burnout will endure in ministry. Preachers are, of course, just as human as everyone else and the rigors of the preaching life require healthy patterns of *s*leep, *h*obbies, *e*xercise, and *d*evotions.

SLEEP

The hours of sleep one enjoys before midnight are the most refreshing. Early in my ministry, I was a night owl. But that pattern took its toll on my body. As my responsibility increased, the earlier I had to rise in the morning just to keep up with my increasing responsibilities. No more sleeping in until 7:00 or 8:00 a.m. For a while, I was burning the candle at both ends by rising between 5:30 and 6:00 a.m., and going to sleep between 11:00 and midnight. Eventually, I made an attempt to be in bed between 9:00 and 10:00 p.m. so that I could get a good night's sleep before waking up around 6:00 a.m. When I maintain this sleep pattern, my body feels rested, my mind is more alert, and the creative juices flow as I engage in the sermon preparation process. Don't underestimate the value of sleep for creative sermon development and energetic sermon delivery. The Saturday night nerves make falling asleep a challenge for some preachers. If you hop in bed at 9:00 and don't fall asleep until 11:00 because of nerves, at least your body will be rested and ready to stand up tall as you proclaim Christ the next morning.

HOBBIES

Some pastors, almost as a badge of honor, refuse to have a hobby. They're too busy building the church and saving the world to have a hobby. Perhaps I'm less spiritual, but I enjoy a hobby or two as a release valve to free my mind briefly from the pressures of life and ministry. I recognize that hobbies can become a cover for laziness in ministry. Hobbies can also turn into idols that we run to for escape and peace, forgetting that God is the dispenser of those treasures. A hobby is healthy when it is neither an idol nor an excuse.

One of my favorite hobbies is fly-fishing. When ministry pressures are building or the church is in a busy season like Advent or Lent, I find that a couple of hours standing in the stream casting flies to trout refreshes me, even if I don't catch any fish. Golfing with a few buddies can also rejuvenate my soul, despite the frustration of trying to hit that tiny white ball into that slightly larger hole. Golf, I have discovered, only refreshes me when I don't care how poorly I play. When I start to care about my game too much, golf quickly leads to the stress that defeats the purpose of the hobby. The goal is to find a hobby that refreshes you. It should be something that is relatively stress-free and allows you to forget, at least for a few hours, the struggles and strains of life and ministry.

EXERCISE

During one of the busiest and most challenging years of my ministry, I gained nearly twenty pounds. I was trying to lead a struggling but potential-laden church in making a turnaround toward vital mission in the community. As is almost always the case with change, conflict ensued and meetings increased. Progress was an uphill climb, and I was exhausted. One of the first things that fell by the neglected wayside was my exercise routine. The weight piled on, and my energy level diminished, which only compounded my discouragement. One of the ways to combat weight gain, limited energy, and debilitating depression is to schedule and commit to an exercise plan. Engaging in exercises like jogging, weight training, racquetball, tennis, or swimming, to name a few possibilities, for thirty to sixty minutes, four times per week, is an effective remedy for depressed, exhausted, and out-of-shape preachers.

DEVOTIONS

Not only is the preacher tempted to let the body go when ministry gets busy and life becomes stressful, but preachers are also too willing to forego the feeding of their own souls in order to focus exclusively on feeding the souls of others. The primary problem with this pattern is that preachers who neglect their own souls have little energy, creativity, and passion to address the soul needs of others. In Mark 3:14, we read that Jesus "appointed twelve—designating them apostles—that they might be with him and that he might send them out to preach." This is a clear reminder that the first calling of the preacher is to be with Jesus and the second is to preach. I'm convinced that the best preachers are those who have honed the habit of simply being with and enjoying Jesus. Can you commit to spending at least thirty minutes each day intentionally and intimately being with Jesus? What spiritual disciplines, books, and other resources will most cultivate the soil of your soul for the rain (and reign) of Christ? If you are a person who likes variety, incorporate a variety of tools to help you connect with Christ. If, on the other hand, you like routine, then select a devotional tool that you can engage daily.

TAKE CARE

Preachers are called to dive redemptively deep into the pain, angst, junk, hopes, dreams, and potential of humanity. If we refuse to S.H.E.D., our mind, body, and soul will experience diminished health and vitality. When the mind, body, and soul of the preacher suffer, the preacher's ministry to the congregation suffers too. So, do your family and congregation a favor: take care of yourself.

EXERCISES

1. Which component of the S.H.E.D. plan have you most frequently neglected? What biblical and theological insights can reinforce the importance of S.H.E.D.-ding?

2. Develop a S.H.E.D. plan. Maybe you can try an experiment in which you sleep from 9:30 p.m. to 6:00 a.m. for seven straight nights and observe the difference in your energy and creativity levels. Designate a day at least every two weeks to enjoy a hobby. Detail an exercise plan that will guide you four times per week for thirty to sixty minutes each time. Decide on a devotional plan to feed your soul daily for at least thirty to sixty minutes each day. Go ahead and schedule this S.H.E.D. plan on your calendar. You, your family, and your congregation will be so glad you did.

7

OVERCOMING THE MONDAY MORNING BLUES

Preachers often experience the Monday Morning Blues (MMBs). "Blues" is a euphemism for the regret, feelings of failure, emotional exhaustion, and discouragement that often surface in the preacher after the preaching event. These blues drain the preaching joy from the preacher and make him or her vulnerable to various temptations. For years, I took Mondays off, as many pastors do, which actually gave more space for the blues to paralyze and devour me. At times, I would stay home alone and pull the covers over my head, immersed in depression. Isolation and idleness is a dangerous combination. "It is not good for [a person] to be alone" (Gen. 2:18), especially if that person happens to be a preacher fighting the MMBs.

The following strategy can help the preacher win the battle against the blues.

PRAY ABOUT THE SERMON

One of the most helpful habits I adopted to overcome the MMBs was praying as soon as possible after the preaching event.

After conversing with people following the service and usually before heading home, I would find a quiet place in the church to pray. I would simply thank God for the chance to preach and ask him to use my less-than-perfect sermon to inspire his people to love and serve him better. I had released my regrets and concerns to God instead of allowing them to fester and grow until Monday morning. Admittedly, praying didn't take away the MMBs entirely, but in ways I don't fully understand, it diminished their power.

WORK ON MONDAYS

Working on Mondays may seem like a counterintuitive way to fight the blues. However, having office hours forces you to get out of the bed and the house. This way you don't have time to be absorbed and swallowed up by regrets from the day before. You might also be reminded when you show up for work that God is still at work too, building the church through you despite your inadequacies and less-than-stellar sermons. If you do take my advice and work on Mondays, tackle tasks that are as fun as they are productive.

BE WITH PEOPLE

As mentioned, isolation for the preacher trying to overcome the MMBs can do more harm than good. Visit and meet with people in the church who energize and encourage you. Enjoy brunch with one or more of these people at your favorite diner. This will keep you from the hazards of isolation.

DO SOMETHING FUN

Usually I would cut out of work on Mondays by 2:00 or 3:00 in order to go enjoy a hobby or some exercise from my S.H.E.D. plan (see chapter 6). I would grab my fly-fishing pole and head out to a local stream to wade in the creek and hopefully catch some trout. Or, I would golf with a friend or two. Often, I would go to a nearby park with my family and enjoy a picnic dinner. If fun family time couldn't happen in the late afternoon, we would plan a pizza game night in the evening. The key is to plan events you can anticipate on Mondays to help you overcome the MMBs.

EXERCISES

1. Reflect on your experience with the MMBs. Do the blues still get you down or have you learned to overcome them? What habits hinder or help you when it comes to dealing with the MMBs?

2. Implement a plan to overcome the MMBs for the next two weeks. Decide where you will pray immediately following the preaching event. Map out tasks you can do in your office that are enjoyable and productive (organize your library, clean your office, brainstorm for sermon topics and series, find and purchase some good ministry resources online, write some encouraging notes to people). Schedule a breakfast, brunch, or lunch with one or more leaders in the church who energize and encourage you. Plan some fun activities for late afternoon. Then, be sure to work your plan or the MMBs will work you!

PART 2

PEOPLE AND PLACES

8

CONTEXT IS EVERYTHING ... ALMOST

Beyond solid exegesis, sound hermeneutics, and stellar homiletics, there is another element that makes good preaching good. The truth is, sometimes the determining factor behind whether or not the preacher gets a hearing has less to do with the mechanics of preaching and more to do with how well the preacher understands and relates to people in the preaching context.

SAME SERMON, DIFFERENT CONTEXT, FLOP

Here's a case in point. In my first year of full-time ministry after graduating from college, I found myself serving two very different congregations. I was the solo pastor of a small church full of blue collar people in rural New York State. Most of the people who attended the church were over sixty years of age and had no more than a high school education. I also served as the youth pastor of a large church in a college town. There were more than a hundred junior and senior high teens in this youth group. The majority of them were the children of administrators, faculty, and staff at the college. Higher education was *highly* valued. Although my two congregations were only fifteen miles from each other, they were worlds apart in just about every other conceivable way.

These two distinct ministries kept me quite busy. Sometimes I was so busy that I did the unthinkable; I used the same sermon for both groups without making adjustments for one of the two contexts. At times, I used the Sunday sermon from the small senior-saturated church as the message for my midweek youth group gathering. On other occasions, I took my Wednesday message for full-of-life youth and preached it on Sunday morning to those unassuming saintly seniors anticipating their heavenly home-going. Can you say *disconnect*?

This experience taught me a valuable lesson the hard way. I learned that you cannot preach the same sermon in two different preaching contexts and expect to connect substantially with both groups. While seniors and youth may share more in common than we suppose, the sermon must evidence sensitivity to the particular context in which it is preached or it may flop.

EVEN TASTE BUDS ARE CONTEXTUAL

Preaching contexts not only differ based on age, education, and socioeconomics; even taste buds are contextual! I realized this contextual dynamic when I used a sermon metaphor in Australia that previously engaged an American congregation. Australian culture seemed, from my vantage point, very similar to American culture. I preached a sermon on how compassion and action are, like the chocolate and peanut butter of a Reese's peanut butter cup, "two great tastes that taste great together." As I shared my metaphor, one that had connected in my American context, the Australian congregation could not help but give the impression they were disgusted by the thought of putting chocolate and peanut butter together. Combining these two tastes could not possibly be great, in their estimation. My contextual ignorance nullified my metaphorical framing of the sermon and put an even deeper conceptual wedge between the compassion and action I was trying to bring together.

The point is that what makes a sermon good has much to do with whether or not the preacher understands and relates to the context in which it is preached. Regardless of the communication style—conversational, didactic, or prophetic—it must fit the context. The best preachers relate well to various preaching contexts without losing the uniqueness of their preaching.

GOOD ENOUGH FOR PAUL

The apostle Paul recognized the importance of context, which is why he preached differently to Greek Athenians in the town square than he did to Diaspora Jews in the synagogue. Paul realized that preaching gets heard most when our manner and content intersect, as much as possible, with the needs of the people to whom we preach. Context doesn't change the gospel message, just how we develop and deliver it.

PREACHING TO CONTEXT

The difference between a sermon that misses the mark and a sermon the hits the bull's-eye might have more to do with contextualization than exegesis or homiletics. What are the unique needs of the people listening to your sermon for a life-giving word? What are their dreams and fears? What kinds of stories speak most profoundly to them? What are the educational and socioeconomic dynamics that affect them? What familial and societal issucs are challenging them most? These factors and others shape the context of the people to whom we preach and must have some bearing on how we proclaim good news. If they don't, we may end up combining sermonic ingredients that, though appetizing to us, are disgusting to them.

In the next few chapters, we will explore the skills needed to exegete our preaching context. The purpose is to put the gospel in a contextual container from which the people to whom we preach can drink.

EXERCISES

1. Think of a time when you saw a preacher develop a deep contextual connection. What did that preacher say or do that evidences contextual insight and sensitivity?

2. Have you ever experienced a sermon in which the preacher clearly did not connect with the preaching context? What were the signs of disconnection?

3. Reflect on the last time you preached. Did you do anything intentional to connect with the people in that particular context? If so, what did you say or do? If not, what could you have said or done to contextually connect?

9

THE BEST PREACHERS
ARE THE BEST LISTENERS

As part of my doctoral studies, my cohort and I visited Seoul, Korea. We were hosted by the Kwanglim United Methodist Church, one of the largest churches in the world. The church had fifty thousand members at the time. How can church leaders care for and disciple fifty thousand people?

The Korean pastors had a unique way of accomplishing this. The church employed approximately thirty pastors whose primary ministry was to visit the homes of all church members annually. Every one of the fifty thousand members received a visit each year! I had the privilege of observing one of these visits. Shortly after arriving in the member's home, the pastor would sit on the floor, a Korean custom, across from the church member. The pastor invited the member to detail what was going on in his or her life, including any prayer requests. The pastor listened intently. Then, when the member was finished sharing the good, bad, and ugly in his or her life, the pastor preached a ten-minute mini sermon that was tailored specifically toward the needs, questions, and struggles of this particular member. The pastor first listened with his heart, mind, soul, and strength and then spoke with the same.

This experience convinced me that the best preachers are the best listeners. The preacher who lives among the people—listening to their dreams, disappointments, and delights—will be able to preach with profound insight and relevance. There are several ways that a pastor can listen to the congregation at a profound level that fosters profound preaching.

OBSERVATION

Listen to your congregation before, during, and after you preach. If you aren't speaking next Sunday, do this while another pastor preaches. Look around the room and observe the moods of the people. Do people seem anxious, bored, tired, energized, or open? What were their reactions to different parts of the sermon? What parts of the sermon seemed to engage them most? What parts of the sermon seemed to miss the mark? Perhaps you can videotape the congregation during the service so you can observe their reactions after the event.

INTERVIEW

Interview five members per one hundred people in the church you serve who are diverse in terms of age, spiritual maturity, gender, ethnicity, and class. Ask each of them to list three characteristics of good preaching and three that describe bad preaching. If possible, follow up with clarifying questions regarding any ambiguous statements. You can do these interviews via e-mail, phone call, or in person. You may want to use a combination of these interview formats.

SURVEY

If you are going to distribute an open-ended survey to your entire congregation during a worship service, it has to be clear and brief. Try limiting the survey to only three to five questions. What open-ended questions can you ask the entire congregation in a survey that will accurately reveal the preaching needs and preferences of your congregants? Here are a few questions to consider including in your survey to the congregation: Why do you attend church? What three things do you need most right now? How would you describe your relationship with God? What do you hope for from the weekly sermon? How would you describe the preaching in the church?

When you receive all of the data from the survey, consider taking a retreat to reflect on the responses of your people. If you have some researchers in your church, maybe they can analyze and categorize the content from the survey.

Listening long and hard to the needs of people in your congregation will enable you to speak life-transforming truth into their lives with refreshing depth. The best preachers are the best listeners because they scratch where their people itch most.

EXERCISES

1. Read the Sermon on the Mount (Matt. 5–7) and reflect on how the sermon confirms Jesus' insightful awareness of people's deepest needs.

2. Upon completing the observation, interviews, and survey, respond to the following two questions: How must my preaching change? How must my preaching not change?

10

DIVERSITY AWARENESS TRAINING

One of the churches I served as pastor was diverse in every way imaginable. The church existed in a predominantly Caucasian town in northeastern Pennsylvania. During my time at the church, the small town became like a small city with a metropolitan feel. After the September 11, 2001, terrorist attack in New York City, the town became a bedroom community for those wanting out of the city. It didn't take long for the mostly white town to morph into a multi-ethnic context. The church I served began to mirror the diverse complexion represented in our community. We sought and celebrated this diversity, but I quickly became aware that diversity has its homiletic challenges.

The church consisted of Asians, African-Americans, Latinos, Caucasians, and more. Some were from small towns, others from big cities, and still others from rural farming communities. There were wealthy business owners, homeless friends, and everything in between these social class extremes. Like many churches, we had four generations represented in our congregation. Some people were shaped mostly by modernity and others were influenced significantly by trends in postmodernity. We had seasoned saints, new believers, and agnostics. Our people had roots in Baptist, Pentecostal, Presbyterian, Mennonite, Methodist, and Roman Catholic churches. Can you say *diverse*?

Not every church reflects this level of diversity, but every congregation has more variety than often meets the eye. Even if a church consists entirely of white, middle class, fifty-somethings, there will still be some level of diversity among the people. Perhaps the diversity goes beyond the color of skin and social class. A group of people that looks homogenous on the surface might represent a variety of educational levels, political affiliations, and theological convictions. The wise preacher will consider carefully how to speak into the lives of all subgroups without alienating any. Some ecclesiologists and homileticians suggest that preaching effectively to a wide cross section of people is virtually impossible. I shoot back the words of Gabriel to Mary: "For nothing is impossible with God" (Luke 1:37). If God can send the Christ through a virgin peasant named Mary for "all the people" (2:10), then he can certainly birth a sermon through the likes of us that speaks into the lives of "all the people" within our churches.

The following steps can help you become more aware of the diverse subgroups within your church, their unique preaching needs, and how you can effectively proclaim "good news of great joy that will be for all the people" (2:10).

CONSIDER THE SUBGROUPS

Think of all the major subgroups within your congregation in terms of age, ethnicity, socioeconomics, and spiritual maturity. Who seems to be the representative for each group? If a major subgroup, say young adults ages eighteen to thirty, is diminishing in the church you serve, find out why. If one of the subgroups is rapidly growing, explore why it's happening.

MEET WITH REPRESENTATIVES

Arrange for a one-on-one meeting with a representative from each subgroup. Here are a few sample questions to ask, preferably over a meal since it tends to foster relational trust and honesty: How would you describe the preaching needs and preferences of your ethnic, generational, or socioeconomic group? How does preaching at our church connect with these needs and preferences? How does preaching at our church overlook these needs and preferences? Be careful how you word these questions since you don't want the meeting to do more harm than good. Keep the meeting positive and let the representatives from each subgroup know that their feedback is appreciated and will be processed.

SUMMARIZE THE CONVERSATION

As soon as each meeting with a subgroup representative concludes, record your notes from the conversation. Document what you learned about each subgroup regarding their preaching preferences. Try to summarize the preaching insights from each conversation with no more than three to five bullet points. Also, reflect on the cultural differences and similarities between you and the subgroups of your church. For example, what are the different and similar preaching needs between you and the seniors in your congregation?

SHARE WITH LEADERS

Don't keep all of the learning gleaned from your diversity awareness training to yourself; share it in your meetings with staff, board, and other ministry leaders. Ask these leaders to explore with you some of the preaching implications that surface from your conversations. You can have a gathering of all the leaders to share and discuss your findings.

EXERCISES

1. How does your understanding of the unity and diversity within the Trinity impact your perspective concerning the unity and diversity within the local church?

2. What three immediate changes will you make to your preaching in order to more effectively proclaim good news to "all the people" who show up hungry to hear the Word of God come through your sermons? Is there a subgroup that may be overlooked in the preaching of your church?

11

LISTENER LISTENING STYLES

Researchers have explored the multiple and varied ways people process what they hear. The sermon must evidence sensitivity to those multiple listening styles. My preferred style of preaching is more narrative than linear (see chapter 22). I also prefer to preach textually more than topically (see chapter 21). The only problem with my preferences is that they center on me, the preacher, and not the needs of the people to whom I preach. Sometimes we preachers promote our personal style from preference to principle without even realizing we're doing it. Our preferred preaching style does matter but not nearly as much as the listening and learning styles of the people who listen to our preaching. Different learning styles lead people toward a variety of primary desires for the preaching event. There are at least four primary desires that listeners have when engaging a sermon.

INFORMATION (MIND)

Some listeners want the sermon to, more than anything else, inform them concerning what the Bible says. People who want to be in the biblical "know" care about the meaning of words and the historical background of the text you're preaching. You can see these listeners jotting notes when the preacher shares an exegetical pearl from the biblical text being preached. The sermon type that most resonates with people who listen for information is textual-linear (see chapters 21 and 22). That is, they typically want a logical sermon outline with clear points drawn from the deep study of one biblical text. People who listen to the sermon for information want to know more about God and the Bible. Informational sermons tend to be titled as follows: "Three Sources of Conflict in the Corinthian Church" or "Principles of Love According to Ecclesiastes 4:9–12."

INSPIRATION (HEART)

More than a few people listen to the sermon chiefly for inspiration not information. This is not to say the inspirational sermon cannot inform, but the primary aim is to inspire. These listeners want their hearts touched through a message that motivates them to live for Christ in the world. While any sermon type can inspire, a textual-narrative sermon (see chapters 21 and 22) is primarily designed to do so. Some inspirational sermon titles might include: "God Comforts the Brokenhearted," "You Matter to God," or "God Can Use Your Dark Past."

REFLECTION (SOUL)

Those who desire deep theological reflection are similar to listeners who are engaged via information. The distinction is that the information-hungry listeners want to get into the details of the Bible passage, while theologically reflective listeners tend to focus on the forest and not the trees. Since no single text, in most cases, can fully capture a characteristic of God's nature and work, a topical sermon that incorporates several passages is most often necessary. The topical-narrative sermon (see chapters 21 and 22) seems best suited for this. The topical-narrative sermon pieces together different texts or sections of Scripture to present a unified story that highlights who God is and what he does. People who listen to the sermon mostly for theological reflection want to comprehend the nature and purposes of God. Examples of sermon titles in this category might be "Why Is There Pain in a World that a Loving God Created?" "Who Is Jesus?" or "Implications of the Incarnation."

APPLICATION (STRENGTH)

There are people who listen to the sermon for practical wisdom they can apply. They want the sermon to reveal what they can *do* to live for God. These application-oriented listeners are not first and foremost interested in theological introspection and the detailed findings of careful biblical exegesis; they are doers who want the sermon to provide them with practical life-application. The topical-linear sermon (see chapters 21 and 22) seems best suited for this. Here are some sermon titles that might fall into this category: "How to Develop a Christian Marriage" or "Five Insights for the Holy Use of Your Time."

SENSITIVITY TO ALL NEEDS

While each sermon type will likely fit best with only one of the primary listener needs listed above, every sermon can, and perhaps should, evidence sensitivity to these premier needs listeners bring with them into the preaching event. The preaching needs and desires of each listener can change, sometimes week to week. On a given Sunday, a worshiper shows up hungry to reflect on the deeper questions of the soul because coworkers are asking those tough questions. The following week, that same worshiper shows up wanting practical application he or she can embody in a new dating relationship. You get the idea: the preferences of some listeners change on a weekly basis. For this reason, each sermon should connect as much as possible with those who listen for information, inspiration, reflection, and application.

EXERCISES

1. Consider ways that your upcoming sermon can intersect with these four primary preferences of listeners. What parts of your sermon will inform and inspire, as well as make room for reflection and application? Perhaps you will want to designate each move or part of your sermon outline with the words *information, inspiration, reflection,* or *application*. After you do this, you will be able to discern the primary aim of the sermon.

2. Sketch out four month-long sermon series, each designed to primarily address one of the four primary preferences of listeners. The information series can focus on digging into the historical background of a book or character in the Bible. For the inspiration series, locate four narratives in Scripture that are guided by a theme such as comfort, healing, growth, etc. The reflection series can focus on some theological questions or doctrines. The application series can focus on something very practical, such as finances or relationships, for example.

12

PREACHING TO COMMUNITY NEEDS

John Wesley, the eighteenth-century founder of the Methodist movement in England, wrote in one of his journal entries, "I look upon all the world as my parish." I appreciate Wesley's inclusion of not just the people in the church, but also those outside of the church as part of his parish. Local pastors are not only called to serve the people of the church, but the people of the community in which the church exists. If preachers are called to do this, it would make sense for them to get to know the struggles, needs, and hopes represented in their community and address those through sermons. A residual benefit of preaching to community needs is that it inspires church members to invite their community friends to the church. Unfortunately, too many pastors get stuck within the walls of the church building and experience the tunnel vision that makes seeing into the heart of the community difficult.

Imagine you are a detective digging for clues to understand your community. The following process can help you detect community needs and address them through your preaching.

DEVELOP QUESTIONS

Develop a list of eight to twelve questions that will reveal some of the crucial dynamics of your community. Try to articulate questions that can inform your preaching content. Once you finish the list of questions, prioritize them in the order you think will yield the most impact for your preaching to community needs. Here are some possible questions: What is the fastest growing age demographic in my community? What are some of the most pressing needs of this demographic? What is the ethnic makeup of my community? What are some of the significant vices in my community?

FIND ANSWERS

Now, chase down the answers to your community-focused questions. You might be able to find some answers with the help of Census Bureau data on the Internet. You can also contact local government and community service organizations that are often more than happy to answer your questions or direct you to someone who can.

BUILD RELATIONSHIPS

Some of the answers you're looking for will require an insider's perspective. Internet searches and phone conversations will yield some results, but some of the most fruitful findings will come from the personal relationships you develop with influential leaders who know and serve the community. Schedule lunches with local politicians, community service directors, school administrators, fire and police chiefs, and, lastly, pastors who seem to be aware of and are serving community needs. Bring your questions and buy the lunch. Keep the meeting to an hour, and ask the most important questions.

Perhaps your script, when scheduling the meeting, will go something like this: "I'm a pastor who wants to serve the community with you. I've heard that you know and serve this community very well. Can I buy you lunch and pick your brain for no more than an hour (I promise) concerning community needs and how you think a church might meet those needs?" Most public servants will be happy to get together, especially if you buy the meal and pledge to respect their time. The relationships built from these meetings can allow your church to have significant community impact over time. I had one of these meetings with a state representative who, a few months later, invited me to open a session of the Pennsylvania House of Representatives in prayer. That state representative and other community leaders with whom I met began sending people to the church I pastored. They were helping us accomplish our mission.

CRAFT SERMONS

Now that you have a good handle on the needs of people in your community, craft a two- to four-week sermon series that connects those needs to the gospel of Jesus Christ. Be creative, relevant, and, most of all, sure that Jesus is presented as God's answer to the deepest needs of the human race.

PROMOTE SERIES

Paramount to a successful community-focused sermon series is the attendance of people from the community who don't already attend your church. Now that you put together a series that is sure to scratch the itch of people, you need to get the word out about the series. It doesn't take a lot of money to do this. You have already created a network through your phone and face-to-face conversations.

Invite your network of community servants to help you promote the series. Also, unleash the promotional potential of the people in your church. Provide invitation cards that highlight the focus of the series and ask congregants to pass these out in the office, classroom, neighborhood, gym, and other places. You can also create an e-vite, an electronic invitation that can be sent via e-mail. There are many venues through which to promote the series. The key is to find creative and multiple ways to get the word out to people in the community. Perhaps the first Sunday of the series can be a Community Service Sunday in which you invite those who serve the community (fire chief, police captain, politicians, school principals, teachers, and community service organization directors) to attend and receive thanks for the service they provide.

PRAY OFTEN

We often think of prayer as getting God to align with our desires. To the contrary, prayer is really God's way of aligning us with his desires. As you pray throughout the process of preparing to preach to community needs, God will align your heart with his "good, pleasing and perfect will" (Rom. 12:2) for this community-focused, Christ-centered series. Involve your entire congregation in this prayer effort. Consider developing a thirty-day prayer and fasting campaign leading up to the sermon series for the community.

EXERCISES

1. Read and reflect on those Bible passages that most expose God's love for people outside of the church.

2. Create a quarterly timeline with specific dates to tackle the steps above and then go for it!

13

PREACHING DRESS AND SERMON LENGTH

When I preach in a context that is unfamiliar, I always ask two questions that reveal much about the people to whom I will preach: What should I wear and how long should I preach? Preaching dress and sermon length, despite their less than spiritual significance, can help or hinder the reception of the sermon. While some preachers may claim a certain sermon length or style of dress as God-ordained, these considerations are determined more by the preaching context than any other factor.

Sermon length and clothing must not only fit with the people in the preaching context, they must also match the personality of the preacher and the community that surrounds the preaching context. So, whether preaching in the local church I serve or as a guest preacher in unfamiliar territory, I aim to be in close proximity to people in the church, to people in the community around the church, and to my personality in terms of what I wear and how long I preach.

MATCH THE PREACHING CONTEXT

Wherever we preach, we want to be sensitive to the particularities of the context. Although I am quite comfortable wearing jeans while preaching, I wouldn't even think about doing so in a church with a large number of senior citizens. I own a few suits, but I wouldn't dare sport mine when addressing teens or twenty-some-things. I saw a well-known Christian author speak at a conference for mostly mainline pastors. He was a young white man donning dreadlocks and a long skirt-like shirt. His dress did not distract me from the important and impacting message he shared, but it did become an obstacle to several of my colleagues in attendance. It was unfortunate that some allowed the preacher's clothing to keep them from hearing his message, but I wonder if he could have done more to prevent his dress from blocking his gospel message.

Sermon length is another contextual issue. I preached as a guest at a multi-ethnic church in Queens, New York, that asked me to preach a forty-five- to sixty-minute message. The suburban, mostly white congregation in the Midwest that invited me to preach wanted a twenty-five- to thirty-minute sermon. The preacher who stays within the bounds of contextual expectations regarding sermon length is more likely to be heard than the preacher who totally ignores these boundaries.

MATCH THE PREACHER'S PERSONALITY

While ignoring the preaching context is disrespectful, ignoring your personality is inauthentic. As much as possible within the parameters of your context, be yourself. If you are a twenty-three-year-old preacher, my guess is the three-piece suit is not your style even if it fits the context. If you are a seventy-five-year-old preacher, you may not want to wear baggie jeans and a T-shirt, even if that dress aligns with the style of most of the people in the preaching context.

I tend to be a twenty-five- to thirty-minute preacher, perhaps because I am a product of my sitcom culture. Unless I'm invited to speak longer or shorter, this is the sermon length I hit every time. You probably have a default sermon length too, along with convictions to support your *modus operandi*. The point is to know yourself.

When a local church calls me to be their pastor or someone invites me to be a guest preacher, I assume they want me to be me and not a clone of some other preacher. However, being myself is not a license to ignore the context. In some instances, we preachers have to find a compromise between the context and our personality. For example, you may be a jeans-wearing preacher in a congregational context that expects and desires a suit-wearing messenger. Perhaps you can compromise by wearing a shirt and tie without a suit coat. If you prefer to preach twenty-five minutes and the context expects forty-five, perhaps you can stretch to thirty-five. Know yourself; know your context; and preach in a manner that is sensitive to both.

MATCH THE COMMUNITY

As mentioned in the previous chapter, the community around the preaching context matters. If you are a local church pastor, you will likely want to wrestle with the question: What kind of dress would foster a sense of welcome to people in the community who do not yet attend the church? One of the churches I served was attracting people from the lower social classes within the community. Few of them owned or could afford a suit. Our pastoral staff and most lay leaders dressed in a manner that the economically challenged could adopt for themselves.

The preacher must also consider the community when it comes to sermon length. One church I served as pastor was in an area consisting mostly of Roman Catholic churches. Many of the people moving into the community were from a nominal Roman Catholic background. So, most people from the community who visited our church were used to the ten- to fifteen-minute homily of the Roman Catholic liturgy. I didn't want to overly exhaust them with a thirty- to forty-minute sermon so I tended to go about twenty-five minutes, which fit with my "get to the point" personality. The preacher's sermon length and style of dress should not be a needless barrier to community people who visit the church and are processing the decision to return.

EXERCISES

1. Consider how your local church context influences or should influence your sermon length and dress so that you better connect with your people.

2. Ponder how your personality influences or should influence your sermon length and dress so that your preaching is congruent with your unique design.

3. Reflect on the ways your community influences or should influence your sermon length and dress so that you create a hospitable culture for people who may visit the church you serve.

14

INTRODUCING YOUR CONGREGATION

Imagine that a guest preacher is coming to share a message with your congregation. The preacher requests a detailed description of your congregation as a helpful tool for sermon preparation. You feel like you know your congregation so well that you never consciously considered articulating on paper an introduction to your flock. Now, at the request of the guest preacher, you sit down to detail a thorough sketch of the church you serve. Here are some questions to guide your analysis, inform the guest preacher, and, most importantly, help you to really know and speak into the lives of the people who make up your congregation.

ETHNICITY

What is the majority ethnic group in your church?

What other ethnic groups are represented in your church?

What ethnic groups are growing or declining in your church?

GENERATION

What is the predominant twenty-year age span represented in your church (birth to twenty, twenty-one to forty, forty-one to sixty, sixty-one to eighty)?

What is the next largest twenty-year age span represented in your church?

What age spans are growing or declining in your church?

ECONOMICS

What socioeconomic level would most of your people fit within (lower-lower, upper-lower, lower-middle, upper-middle, lower-higher, and higher-higher)?

What is the next largest socioeconomic level represented in your church?

What socioeconomic levels are growing or declining in your church?

EDUCATION

What is the highest level of education that the majority of your adults have experienced (primary, secondary, undergraduate, graduate, or doctorate)?

What is the next level of education represented by most adults in your church?

What education level is growing or declining among the people who attend your church?

SPIRITUALITY

Which category describes most of the adults in your church: agnostic seekers, new believers, or long-time churchgoers?

Which category describes the second largest group in your church: agnostic seekers, new believers, or long-time churchgoers?

Which category is growing or declining in your church: agnostic seekers, new believers, or long-time churchgoers?

BRIDGING THE GAP

Now, consider yourself through the lens of the five categories above. As you reflect on your ethnicity, generation, education, economics, and spirituality, do you match the majority groups in each category? Have you attracted people who are like you? Have you seen an exodus of people from your church who are different from you ethnographically? If so, how can this be avoided in the future? Half the battle of overcoming the ethnographic gap between you and groups within your church is simply being aware of the gap. The second half of the battle, and where the battle is won, is learning to preach in a manner that is sensitive to the ethnographic gaps between you and various subgroups within your church.

One of the ways to bridge the gaps is to spend time with people in your church who are not like you. If you are thirty years old and there is a large subgroup of sixty- to eighty-year-olds, spend time getting to know the people in that demographic. Explore their hopes and dreams, as well as their disappointments and fears, so that you can speak the gospel with precision into their lives. If you were born into an upper-class family, in terms of socioeconomics, and are serving a congregation that has many people living below the poverty line, it is imperative that you initiate contact with and learn from people enduring poverty.

Pastors often experience a gravitational pull toward people in the church who share similar ethnographic features with them. Of course, pastors need friends too. However, if the preacher is going to proclaim the gospel with power and profundity to *all* the people of the church, the pastor needs to explore and understand *all* the people of the church. When proclaiming good news, preachers must "become all things to *all* [people]" (1 Cor. 9:22, emphasis added) without losing the essence of their unique voice.

EXERCISES

1. Describe yourself and your congregation through the lens of the five ethnographic categories listed above. Use no more than two hundred words in each category. The congregational description will come in handy when you have a guest preacher who requests information about your church. More importantly, it will help you reflect on the people to whom you preach and connect more insightfully and intentionally with them. Describing yourself will help you become more aware of the potential gaps that exist between you and the various subgroups within your ministry context.

2. Now, based on the two descriptions, consider how you can preach in a manner that more faithfully bridges the ethnographic gap between you and the various subgroups within your ministry context. How will this information change your preaching?

PART 3

PREPARATION AND PRESENTATION

15

DEVELOPING A SERMON PREPARATION PROCESS

I have an embarrassing confession to make. For the first ten years of my preaching ministry, I did not have a theologically reflective and homiletically insightful sermon preparation process. I used to think, along with many of my preaching colleagues, that having a weekly process for sermon preparation would both stifle my creativity and exhaust my time. To the contrary, having a thoughtful process increases the likelihood of creativity and maximizes my time since I always know what step in the homiletic process is next.

The number of preachers who seem to have a thoughtful and extensive process for sermon preparation is relatively low. As part of my doctoral dissertation, I invited a group of twelve preachers to journey with me for six months using a process I designed for sermon development and delivery. The goal of the project was to enhance the preachers' connection to Christ and to the congregation throughout the homiletic process by incorporating various spiritual disciplines. One of the serendipitous results of the project was that it not only helped the preachers to connect with Christ, but it also gave them, even those who had been preaching for two or three decades, a process they never had for preparing sermons.

Every preacher must develop his or her own sermon preparation process. However, the inclusion of several core elements can foster a process that is faithful to the biblical text, the congregational context, and the homiletic task. A faithful process for developing Christian sermons includes the following considerations.

EXEGESIS

What did God say or do to the *original audience* through the biblical text? In order not to grossly misinterpret a biblical text, the preacher will want to carefully and prayerfully consider how the text was comprehended and appropriated in its historical and literary contexts (see chapter 16). The diligent preacher will explore the use and meaning of words, the sociohistorical background, the literary context, and the genre of the biblical text. Exegetical exercises are a good way to get the ball rolling in the sermon preparation process. So start there. Exegesis is typically the most time-consuming stage in the process. Read the text closely, using word study resources and dictionaries to formulate your observations and questions about the text. Reserve reading the commentary of biblical scholars for later in the exegetical process or it may limit your reflections and findings in the text.

DEVOTION

What is God saying or doing to *me* through the biblical text? While the preacher studies how the text was heard in its original context, the preacher will hear God speak today. Many preachers have been taught to never read the preaching text devotionally or it will skew the preacher's objectivity concerning the biblical text. The assumption is that a preacher cannot read the biblical text devotionally and homiletically at the same time. This, of course, is a phenomenon of modern scientific empiricism, which assumed that truth can only be discovered through objective detachment from the thing being explored (see chapter 4). This divorce, then, between preaching and devotion grew out of cultural conventions rather than Christian convictions. If I told Peter, Paul, Athanasius, and Augustine that they were not allowed to read devotionally from the biblical text on which they would preach, I suspect they would either laugh at or debate with me. I would hope for the former, since all of them could tear me to shreds with their ability to debate.

Invite God to speak into your life through the text on which you will preach. Listen to God's voice through the text by using an ancient devotional practice such as *lectio divina*, which moves from reading to meditating, praying, applying, and contemplating, or a contemporary devotional practice like the popular S.O.A.P., which journeys from the Scripture passage to observations to applications and to prayer. While God is at liberty to speak anything into your life through the text, there is usually some resonance between what God said to the original audience back then and what God is saying to you today. The aim of biblical preaching is to find that resonating thread between the ancient text and the contemporary context.

CONTEXT

What does God want to say and do to the *congregation* through the biblical text? Prayerfully considering how the biblical text intersects with the congregational context can significantly enhance one's sermons. The preacher is tempted to run too quickly from exegesis to sermon writing without carefully mulling over how the congregation will hear or may need to hear the biblical text. The art of homiletics is wedding together biblical exegesis and congregational context in a manner that blurs or, better yet, erases the line between text and context. This erasing is easier said than done. It is most likely to occur for the preacher who spends enough time among people in the congregation to really know them. The best preachers, as I've suggested in chapter 9, are often the best listeners. These preachers have found a way to listen long and hard to the hopes, hurts, dreams, and doubts of the people to whom they preach. This contextual listening enables the preacher to create a sermonic bridge between God's Word and the congregation to whom God is longing to speak.

CREATIVITY

How does God want to speak to his people through the sermon? Preaching is at least as much an art as it is a science (see chapter 4). Good art, to state the obvious, requires a high level of creativity. Why is it that some churches will pour a lot of creativity into various parts of the worship service by developing engaging music, writing indigenous poetry and dramatic presentations, and displaying powerful imagery through the use of props and pictures, while the preaching remains stuck in a stiff and stale box? Where is it written that the sermon must be more like a predictable lecture or boring speech than a work of art? One of the most formidable creativity thieves is the preacher's own fear of "missing the truth" of the biblical text. To an extent, this concern is a healthy one. However, preachers can become so absorbed with getting the biblical text right that we actually get it wrong by missing the artfulness within the text itself. God is wonderfully creative and if our sermons are going to say something about God, as they should, then they ought to be creative too.

Here are some questions to get your creative homiletic juices flowing: What metaphors, images, current events, songs, movies, poetry, or memories can creatively build the sermonic bridge between the realities of the biblical text and the situations represented by your contemporary context? What creative touches in the sermon can inspire people to listen for the Word of God addressed to them? What out-of-the-box sermonic structure can best communicate your content?

FLEXIBLE SEQUENCE

While your sermon preparation process should uniquely fit you and your context, a faithful and fruitful process will include (1) exegesis of the text; (2) reading the text as devotion; (3) discernment of the congregational context; and (4) artful creativity in building the sermonic bridge between the text and the context. These elements also present a recommended, but flexible, sequence in the sermon preparation process.

EXERCISES

1. Consider your weekly routine of sermon preparation. If you don't have a usual process, simply reflect on what you did the last time you preached. Describe your process by listing in order what you do in each step of the homiletic process, when you do each step, how much time you typically spend on each step, and what resources you use in each step. Do some honest reflecting. Try not to list the ideal sermon preparation process (you will do that in one of the exercises below), but sketch out your actual process. In

which area are you strongest and weakest: exegesis, devotion, context, or creativity? What modifications to your sermon preparation process are necessary to maximize your strengths and to minimize your weaknesses?

2. Interview two or three pastors, who preach with power, concerning their sermon preparation process. You could meet with these pastors simultaneously over a lunch that you buy. Take a device to record the conversation, with their permission of course. During the interview, ask the preachers to list, from beginning to end, the steps they take in the process of developing sermons. Find out how much time they spend on each step, as well as their favorite resources for each step. Also, find out when they tackle the various steps in the preparation process during the week. For instance, maybe the preacher does exegetical work on Tuesdays and sermon writing on Thursdays.

3. Based on the analysis of your typical process, the concepts in this chapter, and your interviews with other preachers, develop an ideal sermon preparation process to guide you through the weekly homiletic journey. Then, follow it!

16

EXEGESIS 101

High-quality exegetical insights from the biblical text result from asking probing questions about what's going on *behind, in,* and *before* the text. Preachers who "correctly [handle] the word of truth" (2 Tim. 2:15) carefully consider the truth *behind* the Bible passage (the historical context) and the truth *in* the text (the literary context) before running to the truth *before* the text (the contemporary

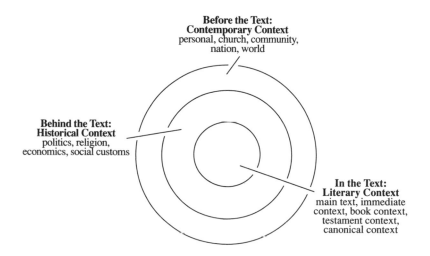

Before the Text:
Contemporary Context
personal, church, community,
nation, world

Behind the Text:
Historical Context
politics, religion,
economics, social customs

In the Text:
Literary Context
main text, immediate
context, book context,
testament context,
canonical context

context). To be sure, the Bible must be carefully interpreted and appropriated in light of the contemporary context. However, when the truth before the text (our personal perspective and contemporary circumstances) becomes the preacher's only interpretive lens, the historical and literary contexts are ignored and the interpretation is badly botched.

IN THE TEXT (LITERARY CONTEXT)

Suppose you are preaching on Mark 10:32–34. The best way to begin your exploration of the text is by closely reading it multiple times while noting your observations, questions that probe those observations, and possible answers to those questions. You may want to make three columns on a document with the headings observations, questions, and possibilities. Work through the biblical text listing observations. These observations are facts about the text. For example, when you read Mark 10:32, you will observe that Jesus and his followers were going "up to Jerusalem." Each observation will elicit questions. You might ask, "Why were they going up to Jerusalem?" Then, you will explore possibilities: "Perhaps they were going up to Jerusalem because there was a Jewish festival that required the attendance of all practicing Jews." You get the idea. Read the text slowly multiple times, observing words, actions, ideas, characters, mood, and flow. Follow each of those observations with questions and possibilities.

After you have thoroughly attended to the main preaching text, it is time to explore the literary context around it. Consider how the passages immediately before and after the main text shed interpretive light on the main text. The immediate context of Mark 10:32–34 is verses 17–31 and 35–52. The immediate context highlights how a wealthy young man and the disciples, James and John, don't seem to "get" Jesus, but a blind guy does. Also note the book context: How does your reading of the entire gospel of Mark inform your interpretation of Mark 10:32–34? The testament context also sheds light on the main text: How does your reading of the New Testament guide your reading of the main text? Finally, allow your mind to race through the canonical context, the entire Bible: How does the entire biblical story shape your perspective on Mark 10:32–34?

BEHIND THE TEXT (HISTORICAL CONTEXT)

There is an entire history behind every Bible passage that is foreign to contemporary readers. Every biblical text is set within the politics, religion, economics, and customs of the time in which it was written. When you do your detailed observation in the text, several questions and possibilities will surface that require you to do some digging behind the text. For example, we observed in Mark 10:32 that Jesus and his disciples "were on their way up to Jerusalem." It would be beneficial to research the political and religious context of Jerusalem during the time of Jesus. What is the significance of Jesus going to Jerusalem to die instead of to some other city? You would do this behind-the-text digging with the help of dictionaries, an atlas, word study tools, and commentary introductions on the book of Mark.

Based on your probing in and behind the text, you may want to write an exegetical summary of the passage. Only after you write this summary should you consult several Bible commentaries dealing with the passage to see how they support or challenge your observations. Commentaries should be utilized to refine, not define, your exegetical work.

BEFORE THE TEXT (CONTEMPORARY CONTEXT)

Now that you have considered the literary and historical contexts of the biblical passage from which you will preach, it is time to reflect on the meaning of the passage in light of the contemporary context *before* the text. The contemporary context is discerned through an exploration of yourself, the church, the community, the nation, and the world. First, consider how the main preaching text intersects with the situations in your life. You may want to engage in a devotional exercise like *lectio divina* (see chapter 17). Next, reflect on what is going on in the lives of the people in the church both individually and corporately: How does this text engage the church's contemporary situation? Finally, consider current realities in your community, nation, and world that are addressed by the main preaching text. Make notes on how the biblical text intersects with you, the church, the community, the nation, and the world. Some of your best sermon metaphors, mantras, illustrations, and applications will flow out of your awareness of intersections between the biblical text and the contemporary context.

AN EXEGETICAL PROCESS

Pray for God's guidance (before the text). Do a detailed observation of the main text (in the text). Explore how the immediate, book, testament, and canonical contexts shed interpretive light on the main preaching text (in the text). Consult dictionaries, word studies, atlases, and commentary introductions to books of the Bible in order to do some digging into the historical context (behind the text). Write your summary of the main text (in the text, behind the text). Consult two or three commentaries on the main preaching text (in the text, behind the text). Consider how the preaching text intersects with the contemporary context of your life, church, community, nation, and world (before the text). Then, articulate the sermon focus and function. There are many possible sermons you could preach from your exploration of the literary, historical, and contemporary contexts—or in, behind, and before the text. At this point, you are ready to decide on the focus and function of this particular sermon. We will consider the importance of sermon focus and function in chapter 18.

EXERCISES

1. Reflect on how the exegetical process above relates to your current process. How does this exegetical process reinforce or challenge your process? Does your exegetical process explore the literary, historical, and contemporary contexts without ignoring any of them?

2. Experiment with the exegetical process above for your next sermon or two. If it helps you to more faithfully build a bridge between the text and your context, great! If not, then try modifying the process to improve it.

17

PREACHING AS A SPIRITUAL DISCIPLINE

When I began preaching as a local church pastor on a weekly basis, I was twenty-three years old. I was awestruck by both the astonishing privilege and daunting responsibility of proclaiming the gospel. I was overwhelmed. The high calling to preach had a purifying effect on my soul. I was more reliant on God throughout the homiletic process than my limited experience and subpar abilities. Prayer and fasting guided me as I wrestled with God for insight into the coming Sunday's text. My need for God was almost as inescapable as my need for air. Preaching was for me, in the earliest days of my pastoral ministry, a spiritual discipline that cultivated a deepening faith in the God whose guiding and anointing I sought intensely.

Then, a strange thing happened. The more I preached, the more comfortable I became with my increasing skills. I began to pray less. Sermon development and delivery was reduced from a spiritual discipline to a technical task. I found my homiletic rhythm by learning *how* to preach. Preaching became a rhetorical technique that overshadowed the spiritual discipline it used to be. What I once viewed as an opportunity to engage and be engaged by God became a task to be completed. This change in perspective eventually diminished for me the joy of preaching and its spiritually formative impact. The frequent result was homiletic fatigue and symptoms of pastoral burnout.

If you have preached for at least a few years, perhaps you can relate to my story. If you are a beginner, you are probably still so overwhelmed by preaching that it forces you deeper and deeper into Christ. I hope you maintain that prayerful posture for as long as you preach. One of the ways to abide in Christ through the homiletic process is to ignore the wrong assumption that the preacher must divorce the devotional life from the preaching life. Reading and studying Scripture to develop a sermon can and should indeed be devotional.

Pastors often bemoan their lack of time for spiritual disciplines. But imagine if the ten to twenty hours it takes to prepare and present sermons could be engaged in as a devotional exercise. Exegetical digging into the biblical text and effective rhetorical devices are crucial to developing faithful sermons, but there are several exercises that can ensure we practice preaching primarily as a spiritual discipline. Try sprinkling the following spiritual disciplines throughout your sermon preparation process.

PRAYERFUL PREPARATION

Before you begin to study the biblical text from which you will preach, pray a small portion of Psalm 119 slowly and reflectively. Ask God for revelation and insight into his Word. Quiet your soul by sitting before God and allowing him to remind you of his love and the important calling he has placed on your life to proclaim Christ. Ask God to purify your preaching motives and spiritually form you through the homiletic process so that you become the "fragrance" of Christ.

PLAYFUL IMAGINATION

Once you have settled on a main text from which you will preach, fast a meal and pray at least thirty minutes for imaginative insight into the text. Read the text slowly, verse by verse, trying to imagine being an observer of the original scene of the text. Try to see, hear, smell, touch, and taste what's going on in the passage. Prayerfully and playfully imagine yourself in the original context of the passage through the eyes of the characters in or behind the text.

INTERNALIZE THE WORD

Memorize the preaching text (or at least a main portion of it). Recite the text aloud when you're alone and rehearse the text in your head while driving in the car or taking a shower. When you internalize the Word, you begin reflecting on the passage subconsciously, and profound insights often surface. One of the ways to internalize the Word is to practice *lectio divina*.

Lectio divina means divine reading. Prayerfully read the preaching passage and consider its implications for your life. Consider what God is saying to you through the text. How does the text apply to your relationships with Christ and others? How does it confirm, challenge, or comfort you? What does it reveal about who Christ is and who you are?

LECTIO

Read the text slowly several times, inviting God to impress on you the word, phrase, or sentence from the text that he most wants to speak to you.

MEDITATIO

Reflect on this word or phrase from the text, and consider its intersection with your life and with other passages of Scripture. What do you sense God is saying to you through this text? Give God some time to speak this word of truth into your life. Be still and let the words from Scripture fill your heart and mind.

ORATIO

Write a prayer of response to God in light of what he has spoken to you. This prayer can be one of adoration, thanksgiving, confession, or intercession, to name a few. Note any changes or commitments you will make to God as a result of being confronted, convicted, comforted, challenged, or confirmed by this biblical text.

CONTEMPLATIO

This final step takes one beyond words and toward images that surface through intimacy with God. Don't focus on words or even the sermon, but simply enjoy intimacy with God, resting in his presence and worshiping him. What do you picture? What images does God allow to surface?

PRAYER WALK

Take a prayer walk around the church campus, your neighborhood, a nearby park, or some woods, looking and praying for God's glory, for his kingdom to come through the sermon. Also, keep an eye out for physical illustrations that highlight the main focus of the sermon.

INTERCESSORY REFLECTIONS

Spend at least thirty to sixty minutes praying through the church directory and any congregational prayer requests, incorporating the preaching text for the week into the prayer as often as possible. Reflect on how the biblical text for the sermon might address the joys, sorrows, hopes, hurts, sins, and dreams of people in your congregation and humanity in general, and pray accordingly. Prayerfully consider how God wants to comfort, confirm, correct, or convict the church through this text. What changes might God want to initiate in your church through this text? Be careful to let God's desires for the church, and not merely your own desires and ambitions, determine the application of the text for the congregation you serve. Don't force the text to say more or less than it really says. List the possible sermon applications that surface from this intercessory prayer time.

CONTACT

Initiate two or three pastoral care contacts via visit, phone call, or e-mail. Contact the people whose lives are most profoundly addressed by the sermon for the coming Sunday. Depending on the circumstances, you may not want them to know that the coming sermon applies to them. This exercise will help you put a face on the sermon as you consider the implications of the text for actual people in your congregation.

FEEDBACK

When you meet with your staff, small group, or family, read the preaching text and ask them to ponder how the text intersects with their lives. What do they observe about the text? What questions do they raise? Ask them to express how the text challenges, comforts, convicts, or confirms them. This exercise allows the preacher to consider multiple perspectives concerning the biblical text for the coming sermon.

JOURNAL A PRAYER

Write out a prayer to God that expresses your hopes for the sermon's impact on you and the congregation. Be transparent with God. Pray this prayer throughout the week leading up to the preaching event.

PRAYERFUL PAUSE

Once you have all the pieces of the sermon (exegetical insights, sermon focus and function, metaphors and mantras, and applications), spend fifteen to thirty minutes prayerfully asking God to guide you in ordering the parts of the sermon so that it will glorify him, communicate clearly, and inspire the church. Preachers tend to rush the structuring of the sermon. We have all the ingredients we want to throw into the sermon mix, but it is imperative that we carefully and prayerfully consider how the parts can be ordered for progressive and seamless flow. Think of the parts of the sermon as a recipe in which some ingredients must come first to prepare the way for later ingredients (see chapter 5). Pray for guidance and wisdom on this often overlooked but vitally important element in the homiletic process that can often make or break a sermon.

PRE-EVENT PRAYER TIME

On the day of the preaching event, pray in the congregational worship space for the purity, love, humility, and grace to help you embody and communicate the sermon through your life. This helps the preacher remember that the sermon applies to the preacher first. After you pray for your own receptivity to the sermon, walk around the sanctuary (if possible) praying for peoples' receptivity to God's Word and their spiritual formation through it.

DEVELOP PRAYER TEAMS

Consider recruiting and empowering the following teams of people to pray:

- Pre-Service: This team will pray with the preacher before the worship service.
- During Service: This team will pray during the sermon.
- Post-Service: After the sermon, this team will intercede for people who desire prayer in response to the message. If no one expresses this desire, this team can simply pray together for the impact of God's Word.

Maybe you can delegate the recruiting of these prayer teams to someone in your church who is passionate about prayer and its prominence in the local church.

THE PREACHING DISCIPLINE

Most of the classic spiritual disciplines of Christianity can be categorized under the umbrellas of prayer, Scripture, or fellowship. Each of the homiletic spiritual disciplines above fit in one or more of these categories. I hope the point of this chapter is, like a good sermon, clear and compelling—the weekly homiletic process will foster substantial joy and form Christlike character in preachers when we engage preaching as a spiritual discipline. Jesus suggests, in John 15, that as long as we the branches abide in him the vine, then we will be faithful, fruitful, and fulfilled in life and ministry. Preaching as a spiritual discipline enables the preacher to abide in Christ throughout the homiletic process.

EXERCISES

1. Pick three or four spiritual disciplines above to practice this week as you develop and deliver your sermon. Follow this pattern for the next few weeks until you have experimented with all twelve spiritual disciplines.

2. After you have experimented with all of the disciplines, decide on which were most helpful and incorporate them regularly into your weekly sermon preparation process.

3. Feel free to explore and develop other homiletic spiritual disciplines to incorporate into your preparation process. Be creative and have fun. Find out how other preachers abide in Christ through the homiletic process.

18

THE PREACHER'S TWO BEST FRIENDS

The apostle Paul asked the Colossian church to pray for clarity in his proclamation of the gospel. He wrote, "Pray that I may proclaim it clearly, as I should" (Col. 4:4). Without clarity, people who hear the sermon walk away not knowing or comprehending what the preacher said. I have been preaching for nearly two decades and have listened to hundreds of sermons from students and seasoned pastors. One of the biggest problems in preaching today is a lack of clarity. When the preacher is not clear on what the sermon is saying, chances are the people who hear the sermon will be fuzzy too. One of my preaching professors used to say, "People who hear your sermon should be able to articulate in one sentence what the sermon said. If they are not clear, it's likely because you the preacher have no idea what you said either. You may have said many good things, but there was no crisp focus to your sermon." Can the people who listen to your sermon articulate in one sentence what the sermon said? Can you?

The preacher who is clear on the sermon focus (what the sermon will say) and the sermon function (what the sermon will do) is more likely to preach a clear and compelling message. Focus and function, concepts emphasized and taught by Thomas Long in his excellent book *The Witness of Preaching*, have the potential to clear the muddy water that exists in too many sermonic streams today. The bridge that enables the preacher to make the move from study of the biblical text to the writing of the sermon, from exegesis to homiletics, is the clarity that focus and function statements foster.

SERMON FOCUS

The focus statement keeps the preacher off of rabbit trails and focused on the sermonic bull's-eye. Focus helps the preacher discern what to include and discard in the sermon. The focus statement is the bridge that flows out of your exegetical work and into the sermon.

SERMON FUNCTION

The function statement is similar. It aligns with the focus statement and highlights what the preacher senses God wants the sermon to do in the lives of listeners. The function statement can range from specific to general. A specific sermon function might be *The sermon will inform listeners on the benefits of participation in the small group ministry of the local church*. A more general function would be *The sermon will inspire listeners to love their enemies as much as they love their friends*. Notice the difference between these two functions. One sermon is designed to inform; the other is designed to inspire. While most sermons should both inform and inspire, one function will predominate. It is up to the preacher, led by the Holy Spirit, to determine what the sermon is ultimately supposed to do.

EXAMPLES

The sermon development pattern, then, looks like this: exegetical summary to focus statement to function statement. The preacher who is clear on these three elements will likely preach clear and compelling sermons. Here are a few examples of how the focus and function statements work together to form a bridge in the sermon's development from exegesis to homiletics.

EXAMPLE 1

TEXT. Mark 10:32–34

EXEGESIS. Jesus committed to go toward Jerusalem although he knew death awaited him there. But he went because that's what his Father asked him to do. Jesus went to stand in the gap between humanity and the sin that devours us. Jesus' selflessness is contrasted to the self-centeredness of the rich young man (Mark 10:17–31), who "went away sad" (10:22) and unwilling to accept the invitation of Jesus to "come [and] follow" (10:21) him to Jerusalem. It is obvious that James and John were not ready to follow Jesus either. Just after Jesus explicitly stated that his mission would lead to death, the sons of Zebedee were absorbed in their self-centered ambition for glory (10:35–45). In contrast to the rich young ruler, James, and John, blind Bartimaeus received his sight and "followed Jesus along the road" (10:52) to Jerusalem.

FOCUS. Joining Jesus in the space between the bullied and the bullies—because that's what God asks us to do—leads to fulfillment from his presence and fruitfulness from his power.

FUNCTION. The sermon will challenge listeners to identify and enter the space between the bullied and the bullies to which God is calling them to go.

EXAMPLE 2

TEXT. Philippians 3:10–14

EXEGESIS. The apostle Paul was an old man stuck in a Roman prison cell because of his refusal to stop talking about Jesus Christ. He had given everything he had to the vocation of building the church but didn't seem to slow down, even in his old age. In this letter to the church at Philippi, Paul wrote twice, "I press on" (vv. 12, 14). Paul did not retire, slow down, or coast, it seems, but pressed on to pursue Christian service and growth until the very end of his life.

FOCUS. True followers of Christ keep finding ways to grow and serve.

FUNCTION. The sermon will encourage listeners to move beyond spiritual apathy toward persistent pursuit of spiritual growth and service.

HELP FROM THE FOUR CS

The focus and function sentences should be clear, concise, connected, and compelling. If the statements are *clear*, there won't be ambiguity or confusion for the preacher and, hopefully after the sermon, for the listeners. You will notice that the example statements above are *concise*, boiling down the essence of the sermon to one sentence each for the focus and function. The focus and function should be *connected* to the exegesis and to each other in obvious ways. Finally, once the statements are articulated, the preacher needs to step back and ask, "Is this sermon focus and function *compelling* enough to warrant a sermon?" If it is, then preach it with all the gusto within you!

EXERCISES

1. Listen to a sermon or two by one of your favorite preachers. Listen for and articulate the focus and function statements. Then do the same with a few of your recent sermons.

2. Preach a sermon with the help of these two best friends of the preacher (focus and function). When you begin the movement in your sermon preparation process from text to context, from exegesis to homiletics, it is the best time to develop the sermon focus and function. These statements should be faithful to the biblical text, but should also guide the sermon toward connecting with the people in your preaching context.

3. Ask five to ten people who will listen to your next sermon to articulate the focus and function. Of course, you will have to explain what you mean by those terms. Remember, focus is what the sermon says, and function is what the sermon does. Compare the lay responses with your intended focus and function. Did they get it? Based on their responses, were you clear enough?

19

THE METAPHOR
AND THE MANTRA

THE METAPHOR

The more varied and frequent the use of illustrations, the more engaging, persuasive, and memorable the sermon will be, right? I practiced this trend for many years until it became painfully obvious that many people were remembering one of my supposedly clever illustrations but forgetting the biblical reality the illustration was intended to evoke. I eventually realized that the use of five to seven varied illustrations, while they may be entertaining and interesting, can cause a sermon to feel disjointed and unclear. One of the ways to avoid this trend and still use illustrative imagery is to develop a prevailing metaphor—the illustrative story or image that is used at various places throughout the sermon to accentuate the sermon's focus.

Where do we find this prevailing metaphor? Many times the metaphorical imagery is right in the text. For example, if you are preaching on Matthew 7:24–27, where Jesus described the difference between the wise man who built his house on the rock and the foolish man who built his house on the sand, your entire sermon could be built (pun intended!) around the metaphor of building. Often times the metaphor will come from a word or phrase in your focus statement. If your focus statement is "Waiting for God is frustrating but formative," perhaps you could use images throughout the sermon that revolve around the single metaphor of waiting. Sometimes the metaphor won't come from the biblical text or the focus statement but from your imagination. An image might surface in your mind that may seem to have little or no connection to your sermon. No matter how ridiculous the image, play with it a bit to see if it intersects in any way with your sermon focus.

Do some brainstorming exercises to help you identify a potential prevailing metaphor. With the focus of your sermon in mind, reflect on childhood memories, hobbies, professions, art and music, history, pop culture, etc. Take a walk, noting objects that you see and mulling over how they relate to your sermon's focus. Read the news, catching up on current events, with the focus in mind. Brainstorming can lead you to a prevailing metaphor that makes your sermon vivid, memorable, and transformational.

THE MANTRA

Another area of weakness in my early preaching was my ignorance of the power of strategic redundancy. For some reason, I assumed that all redundancy is to be avoided like the plague. I used to tell myself, "Don't ever repeat the same idea twice in a sermon. I need to mix up my phrases and find a good thesaurus to help me avoid repeating words." At some point in my preaching journey, I was exposed to preachers who artfully craft a mantra that is repeated strategically, not redundantly, throughout the sermon. The use of the mantra can, like the prevailing metaphor, bring focus and power to the sermon.

The mantra often comes out of the sermon focus statement described in chapter 18. Sometimes the prevailing metaphor can guide the formulation of the mantra. Consider the "I Have a Dream" speech of Martin Luther King, Jr. Through the phrase "I have a dream," King used the metaphor of a dream as a repeated mantra. The speech, delivered by King in 1963, had a powerful and poetic thrust that still challenges and inspires people today. A carefully crafted mantra can be a powerful rhetorical device.

M & M

Simply put, the prevailing metaphor and the repeated mantra can bring the sermon to a higher level. This M & M (metaphor and mantra) combination can save the sermon from becoming overly conceptual and, therefore, vague. When the metaphor and mantra align with the focus statement, listeners will have a difficult time forgetting the sermon. The sermons I still remember years after I hear them effectively used the M & M to capture the hearts, minds, and souls of listeners. Sermons that employ the M & M not only extend the shelf life of their impact, they are more fun to preach.

EXERCISES

1. Listen to some of your favorite preachers, seeking to discern their use of the prevailing metaphor or strategic mantra to bring their sermons to life. Does a metaphorical image or story show up at several points in the sermon? Does the preacher repeat any phrases that bring clarity to the sermon focus?

2. In the next few sermons you preach, try to develop a prevailing metaphor and strategic mantra that flow out of and relate back to the sermon focus.

20

ARTISTIC TOUCHES

Do you ever feel like, despite the truthfulness of the content, your sermon is missing something? Your sermon has clear focus and challenging application, but more is still needed. A touch of artistic expression can spice up your sermon. While I believe the words of the sermon, in their own right, can and should be a form of art, there are other artistic touches the preacher can incorporate to reinforce the sermon's focus. The goal for the inclusion of art forms in the sermon is not entertainment but inspiration.

Artistic touches work best when they reinforce, as opposed to hijack, the core focus of the sermon. Here is an example of how artistic touches might align with the emphasis of the sermon. I was preaching a five-week series of sermons called "The Story that Shapes Us." It was my attempt to help the church explore, comprehend, and appreciate the unified story of the Bible. The five sermons, in order, were titled "Creation," "Corruption," "Salvation," "Mission," and "Restoration." A resident artist from the congregation assisted me with the series. She painted the earth on a black canvas during the Creation sermon and then, for the Corruption sermon,

I actually painted over the beautiful earth she created with black paint. Even with my limited artistic ability, I could handle this one. The artist came back the following week for the Salvation sermon and painted the sun, to align with my play on the phrase "Son of God." For the fourth sermon in the series, Mission, I focused on the mission of the church to "shine like stars in the universe" (Phil. 2:15) and painted stars on the canvas. Finally, during the Restoration sermon, the artist came back and painted the restored creation like she painted in the first week of the series. Our hope was that people not only heard, but actually *saw* the biblical story unfold as one complete meta-narrative.

ART FORMS

"The Story That Shapes Us" series is just one example of how artistic touches can reinforce what the sermon is designed to say and do. The list of possible art forms that can be utilized in the sermon is long, but here are a few: poetry, testimony, video clips, props, painting, pottery, drama, dance, photography, music, sand art, and spoken word.

RULES FOR THE USE OF ART

We don't typically associate rules with art, but every art form is governed by certain rules that are designed not to restrict, but to release the artist. Preachers can benefit from developing helpful rules that govern their use of art in the sermon. Rules are intended not to subdue and stifle artistic expression, but to thoughtfully and theologically guide its use. You will want to develop your own rules for the use of art in sermons, but here are a few to get you started:

- Art should expose not exceed the gospel.
- Art should push the envelope without needlessly offending.
- Art should not be used as a cover for shallow content.
- Art should be employed with excellence and authenticity.
- Art should be homegrown if possible to foster contextuality.

The church has a long history of producing art—especially in the forms of painting, sculpting, and music—in service to Christ. The faithful preacher will perpetuate this tradition.

EXERCISES

1. Develop three to five additional art forms that can be used in your sermons. Think of art forms that would appeal to a variety of senses, generations, ethnic groups, and learning styles in your preaching context.

2. Come up with three to five rules to govern and guide your use of art in sermons.

3. Now, brainstorm for three to five specific artistic expressions (for example, Joe Goodvoice will sing "A Mighty Fortress" after the sermon introduction) that align with the focus of your next sermon. Incorporate the one or two artistic expressions that most reinforce the focus of the sermon.

21

TEXTUAL OR TOPICAL

Preachers lean toward the exclusive use of either textual or topical preaching. The unique strengths of these two sermon types, however, warrant the inclusion of both in our preaching. This chapter presents the strengths of each sermon type to maximize as well as the weaknesses of each to avoid.

DESCRIPTIONS

Textual sermons begin with a specific biblical text to identify the sermon's focus, main point, or big idea. Topical sermons, on the other hand, start with a topic, issue, or question in order to locate the multiple Bible passages that address it. Textual preaching assumes that any passage in the Bible has something relevant to say to the church today. The initiating sermon source is the Bible. Topical preaching starts with a relevant contemporary issue that the preacher takes to the Bible for analysis and resolution. In topical preaching, the initiating sermon source is contemporary needs, questions, and struggles.

Both textual and topical sermons can be expository. Exposition happens when the meaning of a biblical text is exposed. Obviously, deeper exposition can be done when preaching a textual sermon that focuses on one text rather than a topical sermon that incorporates multiple Bible passages. However, even topical sermons can and should expose the meaning of biblical texts. It is possible, then, for all types of sermons to be expository.

TEXTUAL SERMONS

Textual sermons possess some considerable strengths. They tend to seek depth of insight into one particular text. One of the indirect potential strengths of this type is its ability to teach listeners how to draw deep from the wells of Scripture. Textual preaching that allows a biblical text to lead in the homiletic dance can facilitate joyful surprise in the soul of the preacher since he or she does not control where the text will lead or the topics to which the text will speak.

Textual sermons have some possible weaknesses too. They can become so full of exegetical nuggets that listeners struggle to make the connections necessary to live as faithful disciples today. Textual sermons also, by design, present a single slice of the canonical pie and can perhaps miss the forest of the biblical meta-narrative for the trees within a single passage.

TOPICAL SERMONS

Topical sermons seek a breadth, not depth, of insight from multiple biblical texts in response to a topic. Listeners begin to see how different parts of the Bible relate to each other concerning a specific issue or question. Topical sermons are especially helpful when a single text cannot comprehensively educate congregants on topics such as, for example, the Trinity or war.

There are some impending weaknesses with taking the topical route: Topical sermons can become so focused on relevance and practical application that the sermons become theologically anemic, revealing nothing substantial about God; topical sermons can appear shallow—a mile wide and an inch deep; topical sermons have a propensity to focus so much on the forest that they are tempted to ignore, minimize, or misinterpret some of the trees.

THE NEED FOR VARIETY

One of the ways to maximize the strengths of both sermon types and minimize their weaknesses is to integrate both forms throughout your annual preaching plan. Consider alternating each month between a textual and topical series. The textual series might be titled something like "Colossal Claims about Christ in Colossians." You would identify four passages in Colossians that say something significant about Christ and dig deep into one of the texts each week in your month-long series. A topical sermon series might be titled "What Does the Bible Say about . . ." Each week you could explore what the Bible says about a topic such as sexuality, finances, work, or racism. Of course, you will need to explore multiple texts from multiple places in the Bible to address these topics fairly and insightfully.

EXERCISES

1. Get started on developing a textual sermon series. What book of the Bible seems to contain content that most intersects with the needs of your congregation at this time? Why not preach

a month-long textual sermon series focusing on one passage from that book each week. The New Testament Epistles are perfectly designed for such a series.

2. What are the most pressing questions, struggles, and issues that need to be addressed through topical sermons in your church? Think of a topical series that is focused on educating your congregation. Perhaps your church needs an educational topical series on Christology (the preexistence, incarnation, mission, death, resurrection, ascension, intercession, and return of Christ). Perhaps your congregation needs a "What Does the Bible Say about . . ." series that addresses important topics with which people wrestle today. Perhaps your congregation needs a topical series that is focused more on application than information, more on doing than knowing. What does your congregation need to do in order to be more faithful disciples? Perhaps out of this reflection will flow a how-to series on developing a healthy marriage or managing money wisely. Be sure that these life-application sermons are not merely full of good advice about marriage and money, but that they ultimately connect people to Christ, without whom no life-application sermon is worth applying.

22

LINEAR
OR NARRATIVE

Once the preacher has completed the exegetical study of a text, articulated the focus and functions statements, and developed the metaphor or mantra, the preacher must next consider how to structure the sermon for listener impact. Discerning the structural form that best aligns with the biblical text and reinforces the focus of the sermon is one of the most overlooked, yet significant, steps in the homiletic process. The preacher may have all sorts of exegetical nuggets, clever illustrations, and practical applications to convey but can end up throwing it all together haphazardly so that it is choppy and sloppy (see chapter 5), lacking seamless flow and clear intent.

While there are many possible sermon structures to utilize as rhetorical vehicles for carrying your message, most of them can be classified as either linear or narrative. There is a world of difference between the two.

LINEAR LOGIC SERMONS

Linear logic sermons have been extremely popular since the eighteenth century, especially in North America and Europe. The popularity of this form is attributable, in part, to the quest for scientific empiricism that dominated post-Enlightenment modernity. The goal of scientific empiricism is to acquire knowledge by objectively dissecting and analyzing the parts of an object. Linear preaching, an apparent offspring of modernity, seeks to attain knowledge of a biblical text or topic by dissecting the text or texts into parts or points and then analyzing the implications of those parts. This form made good sense in a modern world that sought to explain the whole by reducing it into parts. The desire to know, master, explain, and simplify a biblical text drove the homiletic machine. There are numerous sermon structures that can be developed with linear logic, but here is one of the most common forms:

- Thesis
- Point 1 (proposition/exposition/illustration/application)
- Point 2 (proposition/exposition/illustration/application)
- Point 3 (proposition/exposition/illustration/application)
- Conclusion (or more points)

Linear forms tend to work best with the topical sermon or with a textual sermon that functions primarily to educate the congregation. Linear sermons make sense to people with logical, analytical minds. The points of the linear sermon can be memorable and manageable, if limited to three or four per sermon. This form is easy for preachers to preach and for listeners to hear because of its popularity over the past few centuries.

Along with the strengths noted above, there are weaknesses to the use of linear logic. For starters, the linear point-by-point sermon has been so overused it can appear dull, uninspiring, and pre-dictable. And, as preachers and listeners alike will attest, pre-dictability can cause a sermon to crash before it even takes flight. Another problem with linear forms is their tendency to squeeze the life out of a biblical text by forcing it into a predetermined point-by-point structure that is incongruent with the genre of the text.

The way to prevent throwing out the linear-logic baby with the bathwater is to use a variety of sermonic forms within the linear and narrative categories. The possibilities for structuring the ser-mon are various and plentiful. Try resisting the urge to force every sermon into three points with exposition, illustration, and applica-tion for each.

NARRATIVE LOGIC SERMONS

There has been a shift in the past several decades from what is called the old homiletic (deductive linear sermons) to the new homiletic (inductive narrative sermons). The new homiletic, which started in the 1960s and picked up steam in the 1990s, was a reac-tion to the overuse of the dominant propositional linear sermon described above. The prized result of this reaction was a variety of narrative logic sermon forms.

The power of narrative to engage and inspire listeners is not new. Jesus preached in parables, or stories, because of their ability to elicit the tension that draws listeners into the sermonic event and makes them hungry for the gospel resolution. The parables Jesus preached had a knack for surprising and inspiring listeners. What is more, the parables did not always tie up loose ends with points or propositions but allowed listeners to wrestle with the implica-tions and applications of the parable within the context of their unique journeys with God.

So, what is a narrative sermon anyway? Let me first describe what it is not. A narrative sermon is not merely a few video clips thrown together to support the points the preacher is sharing. That would still be a linear sermon. It is not the stringing together of a few personal stories from the preacher's life to convey a handful of propositional points. That, too, would be a linear sermon. Making points and then illustrating them with a variety of personal stories, though not homiletically diabolical, is not a narrative sermon. No matter how many little narratives are placed within a sermon, the sermon built on a structure of points or propositions still possesses a linear logic overall.

Even if the genre of the main preaching text is narrative, the sermonic form used to carry the message may still be more linear than narrative. Summarizing the narrative of a Bible character like Moses through linear points (for example, Moses prays with passion, Moses obeys with passion, Moses leads with passion) forces a narrative text into a linear sermon that can potentially rob both the text and the sermon of their power.

The narrative structure is not built with points, but with the elements of a good story. Setting, character development, problem, plot, climax, and resolution make for a good story and, I would add, an excellent narrative sermon. Here is one of the most basic narrative sermon forms, which is strikingly different from the more familiar linear form outlined above:

- Setting/Character Development
- Problem
- Plot
- Climax
- Resolution

Narrative has been the most successful mode of communication for inspiring people across cultures and centuries. Most everyone, regardless of age, nation, language, and worldview, loves a good story. The Bible, in its canonical form, really is a unified meta-narrative proclaiming the redemptive story of God's saving love for a world gone mad. Perhaps it is the narrative quality of the Bible that makes it a best-selling book year after year and enables it to cross cultures with relative ease.

LINEAR OR NARRATIVE?

The preaching landscape, especially in the global West, has changed. People today crave not only information, but inspiration; not only knowledge, but an experience. While linear forms are necessary and helpful for communicating information, narrative forms seem best suited for inspiration. The church will always need informative teaching, but my preaching gut tells me that the narrative form has a better chance of opening listeners' hearts so that informative truth can enter in. Using both linear and narrative sermon forms, then, can ensure that the people to whom we preach are being informed and inspired to embody the truth they receive. Simply put, mix up your sermon forms and see the homiletic sparks fly!

EXERCISES

1. Reflect on the last few sermons you preached. Were they built around a linear or narrative logic? Do you prefer one over the other? If so, why is this?

2. Vary the forms for your next four sermons. In the first two weeks, preach the linear logic sermon built on three or four points, with exposition, illustration, and application for each point you

make. Then, in the last two weeks, preach the narrative logic sermon built on setting, problem, plot, climax, and resolution as you weave the story in the biblical text with the story of the contemporary context. Observe the reaction of listeners to both sermons carefully. Consider having ten or more people complete a sermon feedback form each week. Be sure to receive feedback from the same ten people throughout the four-week experiment.

3. As you compile the feedback and reflect on your own observations, consider the following questions: Did the two sermon forms engage listeners at different levels? Do you think the personalities of the listeners have some bearing upon the sermonic form that most engages each of them? Which sermon form elicited the most preaching joy in you?

23

BEGINNING AND ENDING WELL

For most of the twentieth century, aspiring preachers were taught that when it comes to the sermon introduction, "You should tell 'em what you're gonna tell 'em." This often resulted in the deductive sermon in which the preacher revealed the main thesis, or point, at the outset and spent the rest of the time proving that thesis with subpoints. If you tell them in the sermon introduction the most significant insights you're going to tell them throughout the rest of the sermon, chances are that listeners will begin to check out. Their fingers may start texting or their minds will start wandering toward their lunch plans. While there may be room in our homiletic toolbox for this type of sermon introduction on rare occasions, it becomes boring and musty if used too often. The last thing the preacher (and the congregation) wants the sermon introduction to be is dull.

Regarding the sermon conclusion, similar advice has monopolized the preaching landscape. Preachers were taught to, in the sermon conclusion, "Tell 'em what you told 'em." This reduced many conclusions to summaries of what the sermon already said. Some sermons may require an explicit summary during the conclusion.

However, when every conclusion becomes a summarization of what the preacher already said, listeners may leave the preaching event informed but uninspired.

The twenty-first-century context requires a different approach to the beginning and ending of the sermon. Beginning with a thesis and ending with a summary is not the only way or even the best way to bookend sermons today.

INTRODUCTION AND SETTING

Jesus introduced his parables not with a thesis, but with a simile. Jesus began, "The kingdom of heaven is like a man who sowed good seed in his field" (Matt. 13:24). Note that Jesus stated the topic ("kingdom of heaven") and framed it metaphorically ("is like a man who sowed good seed in his field"), but he didn't reveal the bottom line thesis just yet. Instead, he drew listeners into the message by tapping their curiosity concerning the connection between the kingdom and the sower.

Here's what we can learn from Jesus about beginning a sermon.

CONTENT

Name the content. Jesus didn't tell them what he was going to tell them about the content, but he did reveal that his parabolic sermon would be about the kingdom of God.

IMAGERY

Develop a metaphor or image that frames the content. Jesus framed the kingdom of God with the image of a man sowing seed. He didn't reveal all of his cards at the beginning. Instead he created a metaphorical picture of the kingdom of God using the image of a man sowing seed.

CONTEXT

Connect with the context. Jesus preached in an agrarian culture. By using the familiar images of seed and field, he revealed his sensitivity to the context. Jesus used vivid contextually connected images to explore a vague theological concept such as the kingdom of God.

INTRODUCTION BLOOPERS TO OVERCOME

There are several obstacles you will want to avoid in the beginning of the sermon if you want listeners to stay with you through the ending.

NERVOUSNESS

Avoid apologizing for being unprepared or nervous. Most preachers encounter those impossibly busy weeks that limit the time available for sermon preparation. Don't apologize; preach what you have in your heart to preach. Better yet, develop a few sermons now that you can use during those crazy busy weeks. Also, don't apologize for being nervous; this takes people's eyes off of Christ and puts them on you. People will be more concerned for you than for what you have to say to them about God.

SPEECH FILLERS

Avoid the *ums* and *uhs*. Mumbling, bumbling, and stumbling over your words will give the impression that you, the preacher, have no idea where you're going. If you don't seem to know where you're going at the start of the journey, people may not be willing to follow you the rest of the way. Consider memorizing the introduction to overcome this hazard.

SCRIPTURE

Avoid beginning with the reading of the Bible passage. I realize and respect that you may disagree with this advice. The truth is, however, we live at a time when many people in our pews or chairs question the validity or relevance of the Bible. A good introduction, with the help of God's Spirit, must cultivate a hunger in listeners so that they really receive the text when the preacher reads it.

CONCLUSION AND RESOLUTION

Jesus concluded the parable we explored above from Matthew 13:24–30 about the kingdom of God by resolving the tension the sermon prompted. He resolved what would happen to the weeds and wheat, inspiring listeners to be like the wheat. Notice Jesus didn't summarize what he already said. He also resisted presenting an entirely new direction. He simply landed the sermonic plane that took flight in his introduction.

An effective sermon ending will do no less than two things: relieve tension and inspire people.

RELIEVE TENSION

Resolve the tension the sermon elicits. During the introduction and at different points in the sermon, the preacher intentionally causes people to get itchy. The assumption and hope in the hearts of listeners is that the uncomfortable itches, to some extent, will get scratched by the time the sermon is over. The conclusion has to, in some measure, scratch the itch the sermon instigated.

INSPIRE

Inspire people toward decision. This will, no doubt, entail something more creative and profound than simply telling people what you already told them. Summaries, though not without value, are not designed to be inspirational. A solid conclusion should compel people to choose God and the values of his kingdom with greater conviction and commitment than they had before the preaching event. Through the sermon, preachers are called to lead people to the water of the gospel from which, we hope and pray, they will choose to drink. The sermon conclusion is the preacher's final and thoughtful attempt to get the people to drink the life-giving water of Christ.

CONCLUSION BLUNDERS TO AVOID

NEW TOPICS

Avoid introducing a new topic or problem. The sermon, like a good story, should end with some sort of finality or resolution.

CONCLUDING PHRASES

Avoid using the phrase *in conclusion* to begin your ending. The sermon should have such flow, whether using linear or narrative logic (see chapter 22), that the preacher doesn't need to say, "In conclusion" to let people know it's coming. If the sermon has thoughtful linear or narrative flow, listeners should be able to sense when the sermon conclusion is coming.

REPETITION

Avoid stumbling and needless repetition. The conclusion should be crisp and compelling. You may want to write it out word for word and memorize it so that you can end the sermon on a particularly pointed and powerful note.

EXERCISES

1. Identify which one of the sermon introduction and conclusion principles above you struggle with the most. Based on your observations and convictions, are there any introduction and conclusion guidelines you would add to the lists above?

2. Reflect on a sermon introduction and conclusion that had a profound impact upon you as a listener or through you as a preacher. What made each so effective?

24

ILLUMINATING ILLUSTRATIONS

Therefore everyone who hears these words of mine and puts them into practice is like a wise man who built his house on the rock. The rain came down, the streams rose, and the winds blew and beat against that house; yet it did not fall, because it had its foundation on the rock" (Matt. 7:24–25). Jesus concluded his Sermon on the Mount with this imagistic illustration. The illustration accentuates the main direction of the entire sermon: that Jesus' teaching is the best ground on which to build our lives. This illustration does not detract from Jesus' central message, but actually presents a focused lens through which to perceive the primary focus of the sermon. A sermon illustration spoken at the right time and in the right manner can significantly impact those who hear our sermons. Impact occurs when listeners remember not only the illustration but the reality being illustrated.

WHY

An illustration needs to highlight and not hide the point or focus of the sermon. Preachers deal with complicated concepts that seem out of this world. Those concepts, like airplanes, too often fly right over the heads of listeners. An effective illustration grounds the esoteric airplane through the use of vivid, earthy language that paints a picture listeners can see through words.

WHERE

Illustrations are like mosquitoes; they're everywhere. The preacher who walks through life observing, appreciating, and analyzing what's going on in the world will have an abundance of illustrative material from which to illuminate biblical truth. The preacher doesn't need to run to books and websites promising fresh illustrations. Those illustrations are not fresh when thousands of other pastors are using them. Keep in mind that illustrations observed from your perspective do not always have to be about you. Be careful how often you make yourself the victim or the hero in the illustrations you use. Also, you will want to have a diversity of arenas from which you develop illustrations. Explore sports, dating, marriage, family, work, world news, science, history, technology, and medicine, to name just a few. There was a period when my illustrations came mostly from sports, and it frustrated some of the nonathletic people who listened to my sermons. Another way to keep sermons fresh is to vary the emotive responses the illustrations induce. In other words, avoid using illustrations that are always humorous, sad, or intellectually stimulating.

HOW

There are many ways to file illustrations. The goal of filing is to have an organized system for both the storing and retrieving of illustrations. Some preachers I know literally have a big box in which they throw illustrative material. The only problem with this is retrieval. These preachers spend a lot of time trying to find a specific story contained somewhere in their big box. There is a better way.

Create a database or document on your computer for organizing illustrations. These illustrations should be in alphabetical order. Perhaps "Christmas" will be one of your illustration topics. When you come across a story or statistic that fits with Christmas, store it in that category. When you use that illustration be sure to detail below the illustration when and where you used it. If you come across a hard-copy illustration, you can scan and save it into your electronic file.

You may want to consider beginning or ending your workday by journaling something you observed that day. Then, decide under which illustration category your journal entry might fit. If you can develop this habit, in time you will have many illustrations from which to draw without running to a website or book promising "fresh" illustrations to the thousands of preachers who utilize that resource.

WHEN

The placement of an illustration is vital in preaching. When you have been speaking with conceptual language for five minutes or so, throw in some illustrative material that makes the concept more concrete. Also, when you are at a place in the sermon that is pivotal to the sermon focus, you may want to use an illustration that drives the sermon home into the hearts and minds of listeners.

Frequency of use is another important consideration. Too many illustrations in one sermon can cause the sermon to feel choppy; too few illustrations can prevent people from seeing what the sermon seeks to proclaim. One of the most helpful and powerful ways to use an illustration is to thread it through the entire sermon as a prevailing metaphor (see chapter 19). For example, the preacher might begin the sermon telling the story about his first new car to highlight the mint condition of creation "in the beginning." In the middle of the sermon, while the focus is on the fall of humanity and the corruption of the cosmos, the preacher might describe the gradual but complete deterioration of that new car. The preacher concludes with a focus on how Christ came to restore what was lost in the fall. The sermon illustrates how the "car" of our lives can be fully restored and even upgraded. So, as the preacher's sermon moves from creation to corruption to restoration, the story of the car's newness, deterioration, and restoration moves with it.

EXERCISES

1. Develop an illustration filing system or fine-tune the one you currently use. Perhaps you will want to contact a couple of preaching colleagues and ask them how they file sermon illustrations.

2. Commit to writing and storing a personal illustration every day that flows out of your observations of life. Put this daily commitment on your calendar and simply write out one thing you observe each day. Then ask, what might this illustration illustrate? Finally, catalog the illustration in every topic within which it fits.

25

APPROPRIATE APPLICATIONS

Let's face it: sermon application is a slippery slope. At times, we preachers invent specific applications in the sermon that seem not at all related to the claim of the biblical text. When this happens, listeners feel manipulated, coerced, and disrespected. Or, they naïvely follow the preacher down a road of application that is more drawn from the preacher's pet peeves than from Scripture. This slippery slope of sermon application—coupled with the anti-authority, contemporary context in which very few people welcome guidance on what to do—prohibits more and more preachers from casting a specific net of application in the sermon. These preachers fear, and legitimately so, that they might come across as a manipulative authoritarian who pushes listeners away from God.

Preachers can learn to walk the fine line between the two extremes of misconstrued application and no application. The following sequence of considerations can cultivate biblically based and contextually relevant sermon applications.

SUMMARY OF THE TEXT

Once you have done some exegetical digging into the literary and historical contexts of the biblical text (see chapter 16), you should be able to summarize the aim, or claim, of the text. The contemporary application, while not always explicit in the text, should have at least an implicit connection to the text.

SERMON FOCUS AND FUNCTION

The development of clear and concise sentences that declare what the sermon will say (focus) and do (function) is another crucial component in discerning possible applications. The focus and function (see chapter 18) flow out of the biblical text and lead into the sermon. Any application articulated in the sermon should be traceable back to the focus and function, as well as to the summary of the text. If the function is aimed at educating or informing listeners concerning a Christian doctrine, for example, then the application may involve some follow-up study within a small group. Or, suppose the function of the sermon is encouraging listeners to be reconciled with those they have forsaken. A possible application from this function is inviting listeners to initiate contact in order to restore severed relationships.

CONTEXT

Prayerfully reflect on how the summary, focus, and function intersect with the dreams, struggles, hopes, and hurts of the people to whom you preach. What does the sermon invite the listeners in your context to be and do so that they more fully embody God's plans and purposes for their lives? Picture what it would look like for disciples in your particular context to incarnate the realities of the sermon in their home, neighborhood, workplace, school, church, and world. This consideration will likely yield several sermon applications.

CONNECTION TO GOD

There are too many life-application sermons that have absolutely nothing to do with God. These sermons give a lot of helpful advice on topics like finances, marriage, parenting, and time management. The only problem is that some of these sermons can be applied without any relational connection to God or radical commitment to the discipleship journey. The application to these sermons, then, becomes a band-aid that can actually blind people to their need for the ultimate surgery that comes through relationship with Christ. Sermons that continually offer practical advice that is void of God may actually serve to inoculate people to the gospel of Jesus Christ. People certainly need guidance on finances, time management, marriage, and family. However, the wisdom shared by the preacher on these topics should flow out of the Scriptures, profound theological reflection, and the preacher's relationship with God.

When sermon application is grounded in the exegesis of the biblical text, the focus and function of the sermon, the congregational context, and the God who enables preaching in the first place, the preacher can safely navigate this homiletic slippery slope.

EXERCISES

1. Brainstorm for three to five possible applications to your upcoming sermon. Ask yourself, how can the congregation embody the gospel proclaimed in this particular sermon in their home,

school, workplace, neighborhood, church, and world? Now, consider and include in your sermon the one or two applications that most align with the summary of the biblical text, the sermon focus and function, the contemporary context, and the nature and will of God.

2. Once you develop the exegetical summary of the text and the sermon focus and function, share these notes with your staff, board, or a handful of people in the church you serve. Invite them to reflect with you on potential congregational applications that flow out of the sermon's core. Ask them to e-mail their thoughts to you in a day or two.

26

VOICE AND BODY

Christians believe that at a specific point in history God made a major decision to move beyond the mere speaking of words through the law and prophets; he "became flesh and made his dwelling among us" (John 1:14). God's consummate manner of proclaiming good news to the human race was through the embodied existence of Jesus Christ.

Preaching is so much more than just the words of the sermon; preaching, like the incarnation of Christ, is an embodied event. When we preach, we communicate not with our words alone, but with our entire being. In a real way, the spoken words of the sermon are "made flesh" through the preacher's delivery. The delivery of sermonic words is either helped or hindered by the messages sent by the preacher's voice and body.

I had a friend, whom I'll call Joe, who eagerly pursued the call of God to be a pastor in his late thirties. Joe was intelligent and articulate. His sermons were well written and dripping with profundity. He was invited to be the guest preacher at a church he had hoped to pastor someday. While Joe's words were fine-tuned and sermon structure flawless, I doubt that anyone in attendance that day would call the sermon engaging and effective. I watched from the back pew as people began checking out, shuffling papers, looking at their watches, and whispering to each other only fifteen minutes into the sermon. Despite his solid content, Joe did not connect. He read his masterful manuscript word for word, made limited eye contact, and kept his hands to his side or clutched the pulpit the entire time. The church did not consider him a viable candidate to be their next pastor.

Joe's situation illustrates an important dynamic in preaching. Good content without good delivery diminishes the good content. Of course, good delivery with shallow content is mere entertainment. However, many preachers have something substantial to say but don't get heard because of the manner in which they say it. These preachers are often excellent wordsmiths, but they forget that preaching is an embodied event in which the words of the sermon are either hindered or helped by the preacher's voice and body.

Recognizing that sermons are not just proclaimed with words but through the voice and body of the preacher is half the battle. The other half is developing some strategies to guide the use of the voice and body. The following principles can facilitate solid sermon delivery.

MATCH THE WORDS OF THE SERMON

Most of us can recall a preacher who was frowning or scowling when talking about the gracious love of God or smiling while talking about the starvation of children in an African village. In these instances, the words of the sermon and the preacher's face are communicating two different messages, the verbal and the nonverbal.

Or, maybe you have heard a preacher's words invite people into relationship with Christ while the preacher's monotone voice communicated, "I can't wait to go home and take a nap." The preacher needs to be completely "in the moment" so that the body, voice, and words work congruently with each other.

MATCH THE PERSONALITY OF THE PREACHER

I have observed some preachers who become a completely different person once they step up to preach. While this personality change may be permitted and even expected in some congregational contexts, I suspect that most people who attend local churches want their pastor to preach in a manner that is authentic to their pastor's personality. Although your gestures and voice should perhaps be more deliberate when you preach, be sure to let the word of God come through your unique and authentic embodiment and not that of your favorite preacher. Your voice and body in the preaching event should bear noticeable resemblance to your personality when you're not preaching.

MATCH THE CONGREGATIONAL CONTEXT

Like the preacher, every church has a unique personality. Some congregations are expressive; some are more reserved; some welcome the sweating and screaming of the preacher and some do not. While the preacher must be authentic, the preacher must also be sensitive to the congregational context. Don't throw your personality out the window and become someone else; that would be inauthentic. However, sensitivity to the congregational context will guide the preacher in adapting delivery to the context without foregoing authenticity.

EXERCISES

1. Interview seven to ten diverse people from the church you serve and ask them to answer the following questions: When it comes to the preacher's voice (projection, pitch, tone, and pacing), what can help or hinder the sermon? When it comes to the preacher's body (hands, face, eyes, movement, posture), what can help or hinder the sermon? You can do these interviews over the phone, face-to-face, or via e-mail. Figure out a way to tabulate the results so that you can see any patterns in the sermon delivery preferences of your people.

2. Certainly you have some sermon delivery convictions of your own. Reflecting on your delivery convictions, the preferences of the people you interviewed, and my general guidelines above, develop your top ten sermon delivery guidelines. Be sure that rules pertaining to the use of both your voice *and* body are included. You may want to tailor these guidelines toward areas for improvement concerning your specific tendencies in sermon delivery. For example, if you tend toward a monotone delivery, one of your rules might be "Good delivery will incorporate a range of voice tones in a given sermon to reinforce the words."

3. Now, here's the fun part. View someone, preferably yourself, preaching a sermon. As you view the sermon video, assign a grade on a scale of one (weak) to ten (strong) for every one of your ten sermon delivery guidelines. Include a one- or two-sentence rationale for your grade. Let's say that one of your rules is "A preacher should never put both hands in pockets at the same time." Since the preacher you viewed did not comply with this guideline, you give that preacher a grade of five and include the following one-sentence rationale: "The preacher put both hands in pockets two times during the sermon." Your sermon delivery guidelines must be specific enough for you to rate the delivery on a scale of one to ten.

27

PRACTICE YOUR PREACHING

You have finished writing your sermon. You know what you are going to say. The sermon evidences clarity and creativity. Your work is complete, and it's only Friday! You can put away your manuscript and simply rise up to preach your well-developed sermon on Sunday, right? Not so fast. While you may know *what* to say, it is vitally important to spend time considering *how* you will say what you are going to say. According to communication theorists, human communication is based not only on what we say, but also how we say it. Wise preachers will devote adequate time between the completion of the sermon and the actual preaching event to reflect on how they will say what God has called them to say to their congregations. In other words, preachers will want to practice what they preach.

You can adapt the following process to fit your personality, years of experience, and preferences. I often begin the process of practicing the sermon on Saturday instead of Sunday morning so that it has a longer gestation period in which to permeate my soul.

SATURDAY: NINETY MINUTES

READ IT

Prayerfully read your sermon in silence. Begin this step with a prayer to God for guidance and anointing to proclaim his word with the grace and truth of Jesus Christ. Then, read the sermon outline or manuscript silently, slowly, and prayerfully. Try reading through the sermon two or three times to get a sense of the sermon's flow and the communicative tone that will best match your content. As you read the sermon, try to identify the seven to ten moves, or parts, of your sermon structure.

SPEAK IT

Speak your sermon aloud, reflecting on the use of your body and voice. As you speak the words of the sermon, discern how your body and voice can reinforce the words. Imagine your way into the preaching event. Picture the faces of the people and the situations in which they find themselves. What are the deepest needs, burdens, and hopes that your congregants carry in their hearts? Certain words of your sermon will need to be communicated with an enthusiastic tone and sweeping gestures. Other words you preach will need a soft tone and subtle gestures. Imagining your people and speaking the sermon aloud will give you a sense of the voice tones and body gestures necessary to reinforce the words of the sermon.

PREACH IT

Preach your sermon with your body and voice. You have prayerfully reflected on the words of the sermon and the best way to embody it with gestures and voice. Now it's time to stand up and preach it. Some might view this practicing of the sermon as theatrical or, worse, unspiritual. On the contrary, investing prayerful thought, time, and energy to prepare for delivering a message from God to the people he loves may be one of the preacher's most spiritual disciplines.

SUNDAY: NINETY MINUTES

PRAY

Pray about the preaching event. Most preachers are awake several hours before the Sunday service begins. This time can be used to connect with God concerning the preaching event. Acknowledge your need for God. Invite him to transform your life and the lives of people in your church through the preaching event. Of course, you have been breathing prayers to God like this throughout the homiletic process, but now that you know what you're going to say and how you will say it, you can pray with greater precision.

MEMORIZE

Rehearse the sermon in your head. Think through the words of the sermon, recalling how you will use your voice and body to reinforce those words. By now you will likely have memorized the sequential flow of the sermon's moves. Now is a good time to memorize the sermon introduction and conclusion so that you can maintain engaging eye contact with listeners.

PREACH

Preach the key parts. If you don't have time to practice preaching the entire sermon again, decide which parts of the sermon are most significant. Usually, the key parts include the introduction and conclusion, along with an illuminating illustration. Practice preaching these key parts using no notes at all.

EXERCISES

1. Consider how the process above is similar to or different from what you already do to practice what you preach. How has your process of practicing the sermon changed over the years of your preaching ministry?

2. Adopt or adapt this process for the next three or four sermons you preach. After this trial period, reflect on the following questions: Did you enjoy the preaching event more because you practiced what you preached? Did your congregation notice a change in your sermon delivery? If so, what changes did they observe? Did the process of practicing the sermon free you to engage listeners in a heightened manner during the preaching event?

28

MIND MAPPING

In order for the preacher to internalize and visualize the thousands of words from the sermon, a new way of conceiving the sermon may be necessary. Imagine if you could actually see the sermon as a complete picture on a single page instead of as a seven- to ten-page document full of so many words you could never internalize them or recall them during the preaching event. The way forward is mind mapping.

Basic mind mapping has been around for thousands of years and has progressed into some advanced forms, but the primary premise is still the same. Transforming concepts and words into a visual picture or map can aid in communication, learning, and recall. Mapping is not only a great way to take notes, cram for a test, and simplify complex concepts; it has the potential to greatly enhance our preaching.

PLANTING THE TREE

Here is one way to practice mind mapping. After you have finished developing your detailed sermon outline or manuscript, draw a tree trunk on a piece of paper. Write the sermon focus, big idea, or main point in the center of the trunk. Now, draw several thick lines out from the top of the trunk, moving left to right. These lines are branches that represent the primary moves or subpoints in your sermon. On each branch, write a single word that best

describes how that branch reveals or reinforces the focus of the tree trunk. You will probably not want to have more than five to seven branches sprouting off of the trunk. Now, off of each branch, draw no more than two to four thinner lines as twigs. On each of these twigs, write a word that helps you recall what you will say about that branch. Try to come up with picturesque, concrete words for your branches and twigs in place of conceptual language.

When you develop a mind map like this one, your ten-page, four-thousand-word sermon becomes a one-page picture consisting of approximately twenty to thirty words. Writing a sermon manuscript is a good practice, but if you mind map, you will eventually boil down your multi-page document to a one-page picture. A mind map not only helps the preacher with recall, but can also foster the clarity and precision that enhance sermons. The preacher can see whether or not a branch or twig really fits with the focus of the sermonic tree and prune as necessary. Additionally, with the visual aid of a mind map, the preacher can more easily discern if and where another branch or twig is needed to complete the sermonic tree.

PLACING THE BRANCHES AND TWIGS

Once you have all the branches and twigs drawn up, prayerfully consider the best ordering of the branches for the sermon. Since we are clock-conscious, left-to-right readers, it makes sense to order the branches from left to right on the tree. When placing the twigs on each branch, you will likely want to order them from the bottom to the top of the branch. Take your time placing the branches and twigs on the tree. They should be placed to facilitate sermon clarity and flow for listeners and sermon recall for the preacher.

PICTURING THE PARTS

If you want to make the mind map even more memorable and picturesque, there is a way. Look at the words you have mapped on the branches and twigs. Try replacing the words with images you draw or, if your artistic ability is limited, cut and paste pictures from the Internet or magazines. If your entire sermon is conceived as images that create one primary picture on a single page, you cannot help but remember and preach the sermon with precision.

PRUNING AND PRODUCING

A mind map enables the sermon to become memorable, manageable, and malleable. What I mean by malleable is "adaptable." If the service is going long because the guy doing announcements or the worship leader become a little too long-winded, you can simply cut one branch or several twigs in your mind or on the one piece of paper you bring to the platform with you. Perhaps you are the guest speaker at a conference and the organizer tells you the worship leader is sick, which means you now have forty instead of twenty minutes to preach your sermon. Find a prayer closet and simply invite God to reveal a few more branches and twigs that may reinforce the focus of the tree.

PRACTICING

Mind mapping requires practice before proficiency is achieved. Stick with it for a few months before you decide whether it is useful for you. In the beginning, you will likely want to mind map from a manuscript. But be prepared to not use everything in the manuscript, since some ideas may seem superfluous to the mind-mapped tree. Have fun. Be creative. Enjoy the freedom that can result from mapping your four-thousand-word manuscript into a one-page picture.

EXERCISES

1. Try mind mapping from the sermon manuscript or outline for your next preaching opportunity. Use the image of the tree, and include a single word on each of the branches and twigs. Spend some time prayerfully internalizing your tree. If the focus of your sermonic tree trunk is clear and compelling, if the branches reinforce the trunk, and if the twigs reinforce the branches, your sermon will powerfully connect with listeners.

2. If you want to take mind mapping even further, try replacing the words of your tree with images you draw or find on the Internet or in magazines.

29

REIMAGINING IMAGINATION

Preachers are often so concerned with correctly interpreting a text that we shy away from the creative use of God-given imagination. Imagination can cause the dead bones of a dry sermon to come alive with power. This chapter presents several practices that have the potential to unleash the power of the preacher's imagination.

In the opinions of more than a few preachers, imagination and preaching, like oil and water, do not mix. "Imagination is for those who write fiction or tell fairytales; I preach the truth," says the preacher. The presumption is that there is no room for human imagination in the truth-telling vocation of preaching. However, if the imagination gives us the capacity to see, hear, feel, taste, and smell what we see, hear, feel, taste, and smell so often by faith alone, it may be one of the most indispensible gifts in the preacher's toolbox. Preachers articulate words to create reality that people can only perceive with the help of a faithful imagination. These preachers help us imagine our way into the biblical text where we find our story within *the* story of God. Without imagination, preaching would be reduced to the restrictive rigidity of mere human logic. The imagination of the preacher helps listeners to reimagine their world through the lens of Christ and his kingdom.

Albert Einstein and Blaise Pascal, scientific and mathematical geniuses, admitted the potential of human imagination to do what logic cannot. Einstein said, "Imagination is more important than knowledge. Knowledge is limited. Imagination encircles the world."[1] Blaise Pascal wrote, "The heart has its own reason which reason does not know."[2] There are ways of knowing that go beyond logic. While our sermons should appeal to the intellect with a degree of logic, they should appeal as well to other realms of knowledge that we access through the sphere of the imagination.

There are ways to cultivate the imagination of the preacher. If a person wants to develop a healthier body, that person will change his or her diet. The preacher who wants to develop imaginative capacity must adopt a new kind of diet as well. There are several habits that can feed and fuel the imagination.

SENSE THE PASSAGE

When you read the biblical text from which you will preach your sermon, use your senses to imagine your way into the passage. If you are preaching from the apostle Paul's letter to the Philippians, for example, sense the scene. See Paul in a Roman prison cell as he wrote the letter to the Philippian church. How does Paul hold his pen? What does he look like? How old is he? Is he bald? Does he have a beard? Is he frail? Are there muscle-bound guards at the cell door? How big is the cell? Can you see other prisoners? What expressions do you see on their faces? What sounds do you hear in the prison? What does the cell smell like? OK, let's not go there. These questions, with the help of your exegetical exploration of the literary and historical contexts, will allow you to

imagine the scene of the biblical text in a manner that brings Paul
and his circumstances to life.

PICTURE THIS

Draw the biblical scene. That's right, draw it. Reflect on the reality the biblical text helps you to imagine. Then, get some crayons,
markers, or a paintbrush and bring it to life. This may seem childish,
but the images you put on paper will stretch your imagination and
help you picture the main biblical text for the sermon. If you feel daring, you could also try to draw each movement in your sermon. If
you have a sermon outline with three or four main points, draw a picture that captures the essence of each one. If you do this exercise, you
may find freedom from your notes during the preaching event since
it's easier to recall four pictures than four thousand words.

WRITE A STORY

Try your hand at writing a short story that parallels the focus of
the sermon you're preaching this week. Your story may be so good
that you even use it in the sermon. Suppose your sermon focus
statement (see chapter 18) is "What comes around from God to us
must go around from us to others." If you were to write a short
story, an allegory of sorts that aligned with this focus, how would
you develop the setting, characters, plot, climax, and conclusion?
Go wild with your imagination!

READ FICTION

Most preachers I know, including me, would rather read a
practical book on developing their homiletic skills than a fictional

work that does not have apparent or immediate ministry benefits. The assumption is that reading the fiction of authors like Agatha Christie, Michael Crichton, John Grisham, C. S. Lewis, Leo Tolstoy, and William Shakespeare is a waste of time. Pastors feel guilty for wasting time reading fiction for fun when our vocation necessitates the wise use of our time. To alleviate your guilt, don't read fiction for fun; read it to enhance your preaching imagination. But I bet you'll have fun anyway!

WATCH AN ADAPTATION

Movies based on books (adaptations) can be illuminating and instructive for the preacher. Like the sermon, these movies are based on a text, called a novel. As the preacher's interpretation of the biblical text becomes the sermon, the film director's interpretation of the novel becomes the movie. Similar to an imaginative and picturesque sermon, an adaptation communicates the realities of the novel through a combination of words (script) and images (cinematography and set design). As you watch the movie, ask yourself: How did the film imaginatively and vividly capture the reality of the novel? On what parts of the novel does the film director focus? What were some out-of-the-box imaginative devices that were developed by the film director? Did the movie director interpret the book in an imaginative manner that connects with contemporary people while at the same time remaining faithful to the original setting of the novel?

EXERCISES

1. Consider why God gave us the capacity for imagination. Why do you think he created us with imaginative capacity? How has God used human imagination for good in the world?

2. The first three habits listed above are designed for immediate use in your upcoming sermons. Try working with one of these habits for each of the next three weeks before trying all of them in preparation for one sermon.

3. The last two habits, reading fiction and watching an adaptation, are designed to enhance your preaching imagination over time. Make a list of four novels you will read over the next year that have been adapted for the big screen. Pick a mix of classic and contemporary works. After you read the books, watch the movies and reflect on the interpretive imagination of the film director. What lessons and principles can you apply to your use of imagination in preaching?

NOTES

1. George Sylvester Vierick, "What Life Means to Einstein: An Interview," *The Saturday Evening Post* (October 26, 1929).

2. Blaise Pascal, *Pensees* (1670), Section 277.

30

NO CLONING

THE PROBLEM

The Internet and cable TV allow aspiring and veteran preachers, as well as the church members who listen to their sermons, to view some of the most popular preachers today. Those who listen to our sermons on a regular basis might even suggest that we preach more like one of those online or TV preachers. Today's technology has made it possible for local church members to be exposed to some of the best preachers in the world, even while sitting in the pews supposedly watching you preach. This trend puts an enormous amount of pressure on the local church pastor to be like one of those well-known preachers. Add to these preaching demands the pressures put on American pastors to be successful, which too often means bigger and better, and it's no wonder many pastors give in to the temptation to become a clone of some popular preacher. The Internet, TV, pastoral insecurity, congregational pressure, and the idolization of success can create a perfect storm that leads a person to clone the delivery style (theatrics) or sermon content (plagiarism) of another preacher.

CLONING SERMON DELIVERY

We can certainly learn from the skills and principles of other preachers. Something another preacher says might even become a sermon seed that germinates in your soul and surfaces in a sermon you develop. But if God and the local church you serve called you to preach, then you should be the one to preach. Your congregation needs to hear your voice, not the voice of some other pastor five states away. You know your sheep better than any well-known preacher knows them. God has given you a unique "voice" to speak into their lives; finding it will unleash limitless preaching joy. God desires to come to your people during the preaching event not only through the biblical text, but also through your voice as it proclaims Christ. Avoid the Moses complex—Moses felt he wasn't qualified to speak to Pharaoh on behalf of God, even though God was the one who called him to do so. Moses said, "I have never been elo-quent. . . . I am slow of speech and tongue. . . . O Lord, please send someone else to do it" (see Ex. 4:10–13). Whenever we imitate another preacher's style, we are in essence saying to God with Moses, "Please send someone else to do it."

CLONING SERMON CONTENT

Another form of cloning that diminishes the integrity and cred-ibility of the preacher revolves around sermon content. The best sermons are birthed through preachers who, similar to Jacob in Genesis, wrestle with an angel for a sermon from the biblical text. In other words, the most profound and passionate sermons develop in preachers who have been engaged by God through a biblical text in a way that causes the preacher to come away personally trans-formed, limping with Jacob. This cannot happen for the preacher who clones another's thoughts by simply downloading, printing, and delivering another preacher's sermon. Developing a sermon that is conceived in you by the Holy Spirit through your engagement with God through the biblical text not only makes for powerful preaching, but also powerful preachers.

YOUR AUTHENTIC VOICE

The word *authenticity* has been used ad nauseam. But, despite the overuse of the word, authenticity really does matter. God wants to incarnate Christ through each preacher's authentic voice. Christ reveals himself to the world through the distinct voices of Matthew, Mark, Luke, and John. And he wants to come to listeners through your authentic voice. You know your church and community context better than any popular preacher viewed on the Internet or TV. God can speak to the church you serve through other voices, and he often does. But God also wants to speak to people through you, which is why he called you to the ministry context in which you find yourself.

EXERCISES

1. Wrestle with the following questions: Why do you think preachers are tempted to clone the delivery or content of other preachers? What do you think makes preachers so vulnerable to this temptation?

2. Engage in some self-exegesis. Preachers skillfully attempt to exegete biblical texts. We probe a specific Bible passage with questions to discern the unique "voice" of that text. Try exegeting yourself as a preacher. What God-given abilities do you have as a preacher? What would most of your listeners say is a major strength of your preaching? How might God want to use your unique

preaching voice, in terms of both sermon content and delivery, to impact those who hear you preach? In other words, why do you think God called you and not someone else to preach in your specific ministry context "for such a time as this"?

31

USE OF HUMOR

Some preachers are naturally funny; others don't have a "funny bone" in their body. Get it? Every preacher, though, has the capacity to add the spice of humor to their sermon recipe. The key is knowing when and how to use humor, as well as when and how not to use it. Humor is, like most elements of preaching, contextually based. Ultimately, the people to whom you preach decide what's funny and what's not. Your preaching context also determines how much humor is appropriate for the sermon. Knowing the contextual expectations regarding humor and knowing yourself can improve your use of homiletic humor.

There are several principles for the use of humor that can be generally applied to most preaching contexts. These principles can assist the preacher who speaks in rural Wisconsin or urban Philadelphia, in America or Zambia, to youth or senior adults.

HOW NOT TO USE HUMOR

AVOID INTRODUCTIONS

Introducing a potentially funny story or joke with "Here's a funny story," or "This is going to crack you up" can be more harmful than humorous. If people do not laugh, you can lose credibility and confidence. Humor does not need an introduction, as if it is some unfamiliar guest preacher. If it's funny, it will stand on its own. If it's not as funny as you hoped it would be, credibility and confidence can still be salvaged if you don't introduce the intended humor.

BEWARE OF CROSS-CULTURAL HUMOR

Using humor in cross-cultural preaching is extremely challenging. We often project our humor preferences onto the preaching context, assuming that what is funny to us will be funny to them. The preacher can get away with this in the primary context that shapes the preacher but not in a drastically different setting. I had the privilege of preaching at churches in Romania, a country still reeling from the impact of Communism. Church services are sacred but somewhat stiff and stoic. We preached with translators, and when I tried to use humor, I paid for it with blank stares and, on occasion, angry glares. While there are probably several anecdotes and jokes that are universally funny, be aware that humor does not typically cross cultures.

CANNED IS OFTEN CORNY

Canned humor usually starts out with phrases like "The story has been told" or "Three guys are sitting in a boat." People will often laugh at this canned humor, but the preacher's credibility is at least slightly diminished. This diminishment is more probable today due to the Internet, where canned humor can be found in two or three clicks of the mouse. Some people who listen to the preacher's canned humor wonder, "Couldn't the preacher come up with something more original and creative?" Perhaps I am overstating the case, but it seems laypeople would laugh even more if their preacher used creative instead of canned humor.

AVOID INSENSITIVITY

When the content of the message is focused primarily on pain and suffering, humor, if used at all, should be kept to a minimum. I doubt that many preachers used humor in their sermon immediately following the 9/11 terrorist attacks against America in 2001. The seriousness of the situation could potentially be trivialized by the use of humor. There are times when listeners need to wrestle with the grief, pain, and angst of the human condition without humor letting them off the hook. Some events in life and sermons we preach are flat-out not funny.

AVOID STEREOTYPES AND EXTREME SARCASM

Venomous sarcastic humor, the type used in political smear campaign commercials, is all too common among preachers. Because we have the microphone, we are tempted to use it with angry sarcasm aimed at tearing down people or groups who get in our way. Irony is OK, but sarcasm causes listeners to wonder about the integrity of their preacher.

Stereotyping is a form of sarcasm that can do severe damage. I remember hearing a comedian at a large gathering of Christians several years ago. The event occurred during a period of political conflict between France and America. This comedian focused about fifteen minutes of his routine on stereotyping and humiliating French people. One of the people I invited to this gathering of men was a former atheist who recently came to faith in Christ and began attending the church I served as pastor. This new believer happened to be French. Fortunately, this French friend, who was newly transplanted in America, wasn't able to attend the event. At that point in his journey with Christ, I wonder if he would have remained in the church after hearing that *Christian* comedian berate and belittle the French while nearly ten thousand *Christians* laughed their heads off. Not funny!

HOW TO USE HUMOR

FIND IT IN THE TEXT

The Bible is chock-full of funny people, stories, sayings, and ironies. Identify them and make your humorous appeal through them. The humor you locate in the biblical text may have the added benefit of overcoming the cross-cultural challenges cited above.

LAUGH AT YOURSELF

My congregations always seemed to enjoy when I made fun of my inability to fix things or my tendency to mistake the gender of infants. They seemed to enjoy stories about me goofing up, making a mess, or looking foolish. Preachers who can laugh at themselves are usually funny. However, self-deprecating humor can be taken too far. Use it sparingly, or listeners may perceive it as a sign of the preacher's insecurity and may not take him or her seriously at all.

TEAR DOWN WALLS

As a general rule, when a sermon topic might elicit a knee-jerk response of defensiveness in listeners, use humor. If you are preaching on the topic of finances, sexual purity, or marital health, use humor that draws people into the hard truth you are compelled to proclaim. Laughter chips away at the walls of resistance in our hearts. This is why stand-up comedians get away with the crudest, most offensive jokes.

CONNECT TO THE FOCUS

If you are preaching a sermon focused primarily on teaching people how to pray, for example, you could tell them about the little girl who prayed that her tyrannical older brother would be given up for adoption. People will laugh and then you could talk about how Jesus invites us to pray for our enemies, but not like the little girl prayed for her brother. When a humorous anecdote is connected to the main emphasis of the sermon, people not only remember the humor, they also recall the focus of the sermon.

IDENTIFY WITH THE MONOTONY IN LIFE

Find the humor in the repetitive, seemingly mundane activities of life, such as brushing teeth, getting dressed, driving to work, shopping for groceries, cooking dinner, pumping gas, or reading mail. Find a coffee shop and observe people. Watch how people interact, sip their coffee, and play with their phones. But don't stare too long or they will think you're creepy. Consider the humor in marriage and family, dating and friendship, church and career, hobbies and academia. To be effective, our humor must be "earthed" in the contexts where most of our people live.

EXERCISES

1. Review the last two sermons you preached and analyze your use of humor. Based on the guidelines above, when did you use humor appropriatcly or inappropriately?

2. Consider the focus of your upcoming sermon. With the sermon focus in mind and heart, take your notepad to a coffee shop, restaurant, or park and simply observe what's going on around you. Look around, make connections, and find the humor that potentially intersects with your sermon focus.

3. Recall and reflect on two or three of the funniest stories or verses in the Bible. What makes them so funny? How is humor used? What lessons can you learn from biblical authors and characters about using humor?

PART 4

PLANNING AND PROGRESS

32

A WELL-BALANCED DIET

The effects of not having a well-balanced diet can be harmful to the human body. If my body does not get one or more of the nutrients from the basic food groups, it will not fully develop and will be prone to various health problems. The same is true with the church body. If the local church doesn't get the various nutrients necessary for health, it will become imbalanced and prone to all kinds of church diseases.

One of the ways the preacher can facilitate health in the church body is by providing a well-balanced diet of Scripture through a thoughtful preaching plan. Most preachers have their favorite go-to theme, which some might call a soapbox. One of my soapbox themes is obedience. Obedience is a central gospel theme, but if it is the only food group I provide, the church body will miss out on some other vital food groups, such as grace and mercy, for instance. The church disease of legalism might result.

As I reflect on my preaching over the years, I don't believe anyone would accuse me of not teaching sound doctrine, except for maybe the guy who sat in the back pew with his arms crossed all the time.

But I could be accused of not preaching comprehensive doctrine. We preachers, if we're not careful, can get into the habit of a tunnel-vision focus on the three or four doctrines or themes we most want to preach about. If we don't catch ourselves doing this, our congregants might end up misguided or imbalanced in their faith. Do we preach about sin *and* grace, faith *and* works, imparted *and* imputed holiness, justification *and* sanctification, heaven *and* hell? Do we preach from all the various genres and sections of the Bible or just the passages with which we are most comfortable?

Most preaching pastors spend some time, usually in the summer, sketching out a sermon plan for the year. We will explore some ideas for the sermon planning retreat later in this section (chapter 33), but for now, let's consider some ways to provide a well-balanced diet for your local church body.

INCORPORATE A VARIETY OF BIBLICAL GENRES

If I had my way, I would preach entirely from the Gospels of Luke and John. Perhaps you would pick the prophet Jeremiah as the text from which you would preach sermon after sermon, year after year. A well-balanced diet, however, requires the preacher to provide nutrients from the "whole counsel of God." Old Testament genres include law, history, poetry, wisdom, and prophecy. The New Testament contains gospel, history, epistle, and apocalyptic forms of literature. Each genre has a unique richness that can guide and enhance the sermons developed from each of these literary forms.

FOLLOW THE CHRISTIAN CALENDAR

If you follow the Christian calendar, you know that it travels the main roads of the gospel narrative. The two major sections of the sacred calendar, Advent and Lent, consist of ten weeks total and provide helpful direction for the preaching plan. As Christians, we don't just experience a day called Christmas; we celebrate a season called Advent. Advent is the four weeks preceding Christmas that focus on the advent, or coming, of Christ into the world. Lent is the forty-day period leading up to Easter, the celebration of Christ's resurrection from death to life. Repentance that leads to spiritual growth is the focal point of Lent. Generally, Advent is a good time to preach evangelistic messages that talk about the hope and significance of Christ's coming into the world. Lent is the perfect season to preach a discipleship-oriented series of sermons challenging believers to grow toward maturity.

INCLUDE MAJOR CHRISTIAN DOCTRINES AND THEMES

Classic Christian doctrines and themes answer the big questions that the human race has been asking for thousands of years. Preaching on major doctrines can ensure that our sermons have theological substance, that they say something crucial about God and living in relationship with him. Here are some of the Christian doctrines and themes that transcend denominations, ministry styles, and trendy topics: creation, sin, grace, salvation, justification, holiness, restoration, sanctification, mission, and worship. While the essence of a classic Christian doctrine does not change, these doctrines must be articulated in a contextual manner for the specific people to whom we preach. That is, if I am preaching to the youth group on the doctrine of sanctification, I had better describe and apply the doctrine in a manner that connects with the realities of twenty-first-century American teenagers. If I don't, I can expect their minds to wander, their lips to whisper, and their fingers to text.

EXPLORE URGENT TOPICS

Reflect on the needs of your people. What questions are they asking? What struggles are they facing? What dreams are they chasing? Jot down all of the topics you can think of tackling through your preaching plan that result from your reflection. Here are a few topics that seem to have urgent appeal in many contexts: friendship, dating, marriage, parenting, suffering, sex, finances, leadership, loneliness, and depression. Once you develop an extensive topical list, consider distributing it as a survey to the people of your church, asking each of them to circle their two or three preferred sermon topics. Tabulate the results and see what topics rise to the top of the list. You may want to preach on the four to six most urgent topics your congregation identifies. You may want to preach these topics through a Hot Topics series you offer in the heat of the summer, a time when churchgoers struggle to attend weekly worship services on a consistent basis.

STUDY BIBLE CHARACTERS

The Bible is full of characters whose stories highlight important themes and doctrines like sin, grace, hope, destruction, and redemption. There are some rich character studies in every major section of the Bible. The preacher can travel through and teach plenty of Scripture by delving into the lives of Adam, Abraham, Moses, Ruth, David, Esther, Elijah, Mary, Peter, Paul, James, and John.

PREACHING PLAN

As you consider the tips above, you will have more than enough genres, seasons, doctrines, topics, and characters from which to build an annual preaching plan. You might even end up with enough ideas to develop a two-year preaching plan. Whether you develop a one- or two-year plan, remember the goal is a well-balanced diet of Scripture, doctrines, and topics for your particular church body.

EXERCISES

1. Begin to sketch out some immediate sermon or series ideas under each of the categories above.

2. Now, try to develop a one- or two-year preaching plan that provides a well-balanced blend of the biblical narrative, the Christian calendar, important doctrines, and topics that address the unique needs of your congregation.

33

THE SERMON
PLANNING RETREAT

The benefits of a sermon planning retreat make it a worthy use of the preacher's time. Some preachers are not convinced that such a retreat is necessary, while others puzzle over how to plan for a personal retreat of this magnitude. In order to convince the unconvinced and assist the willing, let's explore the rationale, requisites, resources, and regimen for the sermon planning retreat.

RATIONALE

CONNECTION

Preachers need time alone with God to connect with him. This time alone requires the preacher to get away from the hustle and bustle of the church office in order to prayerfully consider the texts and topics through which God may want to speak to the congregation. Setting aside an entire day to, in essence, say to God, "Speak, for your servant is listening," rekindles the preacher's relational connection to Christ and refreshes the soul of the preacher. More to the point, the pastor who frequently retreats to be alone with God for soul refreshment and ministry planning is less likely to experience burnout than the pastor who is constantly running, going, and doing.

CALMNESS

The rigors of preaching on a regular basis are not for the faint of heart. The stress of birthing the sermonic baby week after week can get the best of us. We deliver our baby on Sunday, hoping that everyone in attendance thinks the "kid" is cute, and by Monday we frantically search for another biblical text or topic that will develop in time for labor and delivery the following Sunday. A sermon planning retreat extends the gestation period. It allows sermons an extended time to grow within us. Furthermore, when we preachers know what texts or topics we will address over the next few months, a measure of calmness replaces some of the anxiety.

COORDINATION

One of the fringe benefits of a sermon planning retreat is the long-term sermon plan that enables the church to effectively and adequately promote upcoming sermons and series. Knowing what sermons are coming allows you and the church time to coordinate with other ministries, events, and programs within your church and community. Sermon planning has the potential to enhance the worship vitality of the congregation. Your worship service planning team will appreciate you giving them several months to creatively coordinate worship elements around the theme of the sermon. You can also coordinate your sermon plan with pastoral care. You will likely find yourself in pastoral care conversations in which you let people know that an upcoming sermon or series will be addressing some of the issues they're facing.

REQUISITES

COMMITMENT

Consider scheduling a sermon planning retreat on your calendar every four months so that you can begin to plan for sermons and series at least two months out. So, for example, if you are going to plan for sermons beginning in September, your quarterly sermon planning retreat should take place in late June or early July. This will allow each sermon idea or series at least two months to germinate and penetrate your soul and mind. Schedule these four quarterly retreats before the new year begins and commit to taking them during workdays, not days off. If possible, invite someone else to preach on the weekend following your full-day retreat. If you don't do this, during the retreat you may find your mind wandering away from the quarterly preaching plan and toward the coming Sunday's sermon.

CAVE

Once you commit to the quarterly sermon planning retreats in the year ahead, you can hunt for a cave. This is not a literal cave, of course, but a place where you can hide away and not be easily found. Only your spouse, a key lay leader, and one other staff member should know where to reach you in case of an emergency. Other than that, keep the location a secret. Find a cave that is relatively free from distractions you cannot control (noisy crowds, extreme heat, intense cold) or diversions you cannot resist (TV, excellent cell phone reception, e-mail). Book your cave at least one month in advance.

CONTRITION

It almost goes without saying, but being a preacher I'll say it anyway: Take with you an openness and eagerness to encounter and hear from God. God tends to speak most when we put our-selves in a posture to listen. I don't think I ever came away from one of these retreats without receiving important impressions that resulted from my encounter with God. I didn't always come away pleased with the progress I made on my preaching plan, but I always came away refreshed by God's presence. Contrition comes from recognizing that more important than the work of the Lord is the Lord of the work. A sermon planning retreat, I hope, produces a plan for your upcoming sermons. But, at the end of the day, the best preachers are those who encounter and walk with God. A good sermon planning retreat happens when the preacher connects at a deep level with God, regardless of the progress on the sermon plan.

RESOURCES

CALENDAR

Bring to the retreat a master calendar that lists holy days, holi-days, and local church events for the upcoming quarter. First, you will want to consult the Christian calendar when planning sermons and series. Lent and Advent are two high points that present golden opportunities for sermon series appropriate to the themes of these liturgical seasons. Other holy days you might want to include in your preaching plan are Palm Sunday, Good Friday, and Pentecost Sunday.

You will want the master calendar to also show the dates of sec-ular holidays. New Year's Day, Memorial Day, Independence Day, Labor Day, and Thanksgiving are secular holidays that open up doors to various preaching possibilities.

Finally, be sure to list dates for significant upcoming events in the life of your local church. This way you can discern any possible connections between sermon ideas and big events. Occasions such as baptism, Communion, and membership might warrant particular sermon texts and topics.

CHOW

Unless you're fasting, it is wise to eat a full breakfast before the retreat and to bring some snacks that will keep you alert and energized during the retreat. Two bananas, a thermos of coffee, and several bottles of water do the trick for me. A few sugary sweets can help get the creative juices flowing too.

CONTENTS

Be sure to bring several translations of the Bible with you. You will also want to bring a writing pad, laptop, or some other device on which you can record ideas for series and sermons. Music that inspires you to worship God can foster creativity. Maybe you already have a file of ideas you've been collecting for sermons and series. Bring it. If you don't have this sermon ideas file, you will want to create one on your computer and begin to record the ideas that come to you between retreats.

REGIMEN

As you consider how to structure your sermon planning retreat, consider the following progression.

COMMUNION

My aim at the beginning of the retreat is to simply enjoy communion with God. This is easier said than done. I need time to get beyond the stress and distractions of life and ministry to center my mind and heart on God. One of the ways I do this is to throw on some tranquil instrumental music and read aloud from the Psalms or words of Christ from the Gospels. The Scripture reading usually leads to spontaneous prayers of adoration, confession, thanksgiving, and supplication (ACTS). It usually takes me about sixty to ninety minutes to throw off distraction and genuinely experience communion with God.

CONTEXT

Once I connect with God, I spend some time reflecting on and praying for the people in my congregational context. A congregational directory assists me with this. I want the quarterly sermons to intersect with the deepest needs and questions of the particular people I serve. Therefore, it's imperative that I spend an hour or so prayerfully reflecting on the congregation, as well as the local, national, and global contexts that shape their lives. What is going on in the life of the church that shapes the congregation? What cultural trends are impacting the people? What current events are on the minds of the people? What texts and topics, doctrines and themes, need to be addressed to help the congregation more faithfully love, follow, and serve Christ? You may want to distribute surveys to the people in your church that invite responses to some of the questions above (chapter 35). You can take the compiled data from your congregational survey with you on the retreat. Discernment and prayer regarding congregational needs may take sixty to ninety minutes.

COMMENCE

You have spent time communing with God and prayerfully considering your congregational context. During that time, God was surely giving you impressions and ideas regarding your preaching plan. It is now time to begin sketching out some specifics regarding sermons and series. Go ahead and grab the calendar you brought with you. If you are going to do any series, plug them into the calendar first. Then, if you have any stand-alone sermons, put them on the calendar. Hopefully, you have four months worth of sermon starters. For each sermon, list a working title, text(s), and a theme sentence which begins to capture what the sermon will likely be about. (Note: This is not the focus statement from chapter 18 that you will develop only after thorough engagement with the biblical text.) Add a little more detail to the first two months of the quarterly sermons. Consider listing Christian doctrines, congregational needs, images, illustrations, or metaphors, and possible applications that seem to surface from the texts and topics you will explore. This exercise will take the remainder of the four to six hours you've scheduled for the retreat.

GET STARTED

Schedule your quarterly sermon planning retreats on days you already work. Recruit someone to preach on the Sundays following the week of your retreats so that you're not distracted by the impending sermon and losing sight of the forest for the trees. Approach these retreats not only as an opportunity to plan your sermons, but also as a chance to encounter God in ways that increase your love for him and for the people to whom you preach. Go for it!

EXERCISES

1. Contact two or three other preachers to find out their rationale, requisites, resources, and regimen for the sermon planning retreat. Which of their ideas will you adopt?

2. When you take your sermon planning retreats, invite the leadership of the church to be in prayer for you during that time. Their praying will not only enhance your retreat, it will involve them in this communal event called preaching.

34

THE SERMON
PLANNING TEAM

No matter the size of the church they serve, an increasing number of preachers are developing their annual sermon plan with the help of a creative team. This chapter lays out a process for brainstorming and planning sermon ideas with your team.

Throughout history, the church has made its best decisions in the context of community. As early in the journey of the Christian church as Acts 15, a community of leaders came together to embrace the incorporation of Gentiles into the church. Up to that point, the church was entirely Jewish. From the first century until now, the church has made its wisest strategic decisions when a team of leaders with different perspectives and serving within different contexts were each given a voice. The Apostles' Creed, Nicene Creed, Chalcedonian Creed, and Athanasian Creed are crucial theological statements regarding the identity of Jesus Christ, the nature of the Trinity, and the mission of the church. These momentous creeds were hashed out not by some isolated lone ranger cloistered away in an ivory tower, but by a team of committed and capable people who brought their unique personalities and perspectives to the decision-making table.

Developing a sermon planning team is one way to invite a multiplicity of leaders with a diversity of perspectives to have input
into the sermon planning process. While this certainly decreases
the immediate control of the primary preaching pastor(s), it can be
extremely beneficial in the long run. The benefits are at least two-
fold. First, the sermons you plan with your team will likely be more
creative and contextually relevant than they would be without their
help. Second, people will learn to appreciate and value preaching
even more as they are invited into the sermon planning process.

There are numerous ways to unleash the potential of the sermon planning team. We will explore one possible format. The following format is designed to be utilized in some combination with
the sermon planning retreat described in chapter 33.

RECRUIT

One of the most important factors in developing a high-func-
tioning team is the recruitment of team members. The well-known
three Cs of hiring are character, competence, and chemistry. These
criteria are sufficient for the selection of the sermon planning team
members as well. Recruit people who evidence Christlike character at home, church, and Walmart. Select team members who also
possess Bible and relational competence. Chemistry not only
describes how team members relate to each other, but also how
those members reflect the diversity within the congregation. If
there are seniors, mid-lifers, young adults, and teenagers listening
to your sermons, then for the sake of chemistry you may want to
have each age group represented on your team. If your congregation is made up of African-American, Asian, Hispanic, and Caucasian people, it would be wise for your team to reflect such
diversity. Once you list all the people you can think of in your

church who possess character and competence, as described above, seek to build a team that reflects the chemistry of diversity. When it comes to the number of people on your team, anywhere between five and ten people will work, but seven seems to be ideal.

ROUND UP

Now that you have your team, go ahead and schedule a day to get the team together. Block off a four-hour period for the roundup. This is enough time to break a lot of ground on sermon planning, but not so much time that the group will regret they agreed to be on the team. Try scheduling the meeting on a weekday, since most people tend to guard their weekends. Begin the meeting between 5 and 6 p.m. with a dinner the church provides. The meeting will end between 9 and 10 p.m. If you must meet on the weekend, try meeting Sunday after worship services so that team members won't need to make a separate trip to the church.

You will want to have a well-developed agenda that is strategic and clear so that team members do not feel as if their precious time is being wasted. During the meal, you may want to start with some fun, team-building exercises to facilitate team comfort, connection, and chemistry. After the meal, spend a few minutes praying that God would use the team for his purposes in the life of the church. Then, let the discussion begin! Creatively lead the team in wrestling with the following kinds of contextual questions: Who attends our church? What are their most pressing physical, spiritual, and emotional needs? What are the most prevalent faith and life questions our people are asking? What recent sermons seemed to have the most profound impact on our church and why? If you had to pick five sermon topics for the congregation, what would they be? (You might give team members a list of topics from which to pick.) If you had to pick three Christian doctrines to preach for the congregation, what would they be? (Again, you might give team members a list of doctrines from which to pick.)

As the team responds to these questions, someone will need to take detailed notes. In order not to miss any of the discussion, give the team a few minutes to write out their responses to the questions and audio record the discussion. The team can submit their written reflections to you before leaving the meeting. Be creative and do whatever it takes to tap into the creativity and insightfulness of your team for sermon planning.

RETREAT

After meeting with the sermon planning team, take the personal sermon planning retreat described in chapter 33. Part of the regimen for that retreat involves discerning the preaching needs of the congregational context. That element of your retreat experience will, no doubt, be much richer if you have good notes from your sermon planning team discussion. Your intuitive pulse on the congregation is surely helpful; but imagine how much insight can be gleaned from the team regarding the spiritual needs, hopes, and struggles of the congregation. So, attempt to schedule your team gathering one to two weeks prior to your personal sermon planning retreat.

REGROUP

Try to regroup with your team one to two weeks after your personal sermon planning retreat. You should have scheduled this regroup at the conclusion of your initial roundup described above. During the regroup, supply team members with sermons and series that fill in your quarterly preaching plan. Be sure to show them how their input informed the preaching plan. This regroup session should take only two to three hours. Perhaps this gathering can begin on the same day of the week and at the same time the initial roundup was held. Go with a pizza dinner or something easy for people to eat while engaging in discussion. The goal of this time is to walk through all of the sermons one by one, inviting the input of the group regarding the potential significance of the sermon; illustrations, images, or metaphors; and possible applications of the sermon theme.

EXERCISES

1. Designate dates for the sermon planning team roundup, your personal sermon planning retreat, and the sermon planning team regroup. Try to schedule these events in the order above two weeks apart from each other.

2. Write the names of people in the church you serve who have the character and competence to assist you on the sermon planning team. Be sure to select team members who possess the chemistry of diversity in terms of age, gender, ethnicity, and socioeconomics. Send an e-mail or letter inviting them to participate in the initial roundup you have scheduled.

35

ASK THE FLOCK

Prudent preachers listen attentively to their congregation to identify the texts and topics that most need to be addressed through the annual preaching plan. One of the most effective ways to discern the voice of the people you serve is to develop and distribute a survey that allows them to communicate their preaching needs and hopes.

The sample sermon survey below is designed to reveal the homiletic hungers present within your congregation. You will undoubtedly want to modify it to fit your particular context. The most effective time to distribute the survey is during the corporate worship gathering. Place it in the worship folder or bulletin that people receive on the way into the worship center. If you don't publish a weekly folder or bulletin, simply have your greeters hand the survey to people as they enter the worship center. During the service, perhaps just before the offering is received, give the congregation a few minutes to complete the survey. Completing the survey should take no more than two or three minutes. Have some upbeat, celebrative worship music playing in the background as people complete the survey. The survey should be anonymous

but include a few demographic questions. Here is a sample survey
that can be adapted to your context.

SURVEY

Your spiritual needs matter to us because you matter to us. Please take
a moment to express your sermon interests and needs by completing
this form and placing it in the offering plate later in the service.

Number of years as a follower of Christ:

Number of years at this church:

Your age: 16–25, 26–35, 36–45, 46–55, 56–65, 66–75, 76+

TOPICS

Please circle no more than three topics below that you would like to
see addressed in an upcoming sermon or sermon series.

Addiction	Finances	Leadership	Sex
Compassion	Forgiveness	Marriage	Suffering
Courage	Friendship	Parenting	Temptation
Dating	God's Will	Politics	Use of Time
Depression	Humility	Racism	War
Divorce	Joy	Servanthood	Work

DOCTRINES

Please circle no more than three Christian doctrines below that you
would like to see addressed in an upcoming sermon or sermon series.

- God the Father
- God the Son
- God the Holy Spirit
- The Incarnation (an exploration of God becoming human in Christ)
- The Trinity (an exploration of the nature, interrelationships, and purpose of Father, Son, and Holy Spirit)
- Sin (an exploration of the problem of sin and its consequences)
- The Church (an exploration of the identity and mission of the church in the world)
- The Second Coming (an exploration of the promised return of Christ)

DOCTRINES CONTINUED

- Scripture (an exploration of the nature and purpose of the Bible)
- Spiritual Gifts (an exploration of the gifts God gives to people to fulfill his will)
- Sacraments (an exploration of the nature and purpose of baptism and Communion)

- Heaven
- Hell
- Grace
- Holiness
- Creation
- Prayer

BOOKS OF THE BIBLE

Please circle no more than three books of the Bible that you would like to see addressed in an upcoming sermon or sermon series.

Genesis	Job	Nahum	Colossians
Exodus	Psalms	Habakkuk	1 Thessalonians
Leviticus	Proverbs	Zephaniah	2 Thessalonians
Numbers	Ecclesiastes	Haggai	1 Timothy
Deuteronomy	Song of	Zechariah	2 Timothy
Joshua	Solomon	Malachi	Titus
Judges	Isaiah	Matthew	Philemon
Ruth	Jeremiah	Mark	Hebrews
1 Samuel	Lamentations	Luke	James
2 Samuel	Ezekiel	John	1 Peter
1 Kings	Daniel	Acts	2 Peter
2 Kings	Hosea	Romans	1 John
1 Chronicles	Joel	1 Corinthians	2 John
2 Chronicles	Amos	2 Corinthians	3 John
Ezra	Obadiah	Galatians	Jude
Nehemiah	Jonah	Ephesians	Revelation
Esther	Micah	Philippians	

OTHER

Please list any other sermon topics you would like to see addressed:

_____.

Thank you for taking the time to complete this survey and for showing up hungry to worship and encounter God through the weekly sermon and other parts of the service.

The results from this survey will add an informed spark to your sermon planning retreat (chapter 33) and your sermon planning team meeting (chapter 34). Compiling the results of the survey will simply be a matter of data entry and careful analysis of implications. If you have a numbers-loving layperson or staff member, ask them to tabulate the survey results and save the document to a computer so you can compare survey results year to year.

A careful and prayerful analysis of the survey results should yield insights that help you develop your sermon plan. You may be able to combine a desirable topic with a desirable book of the Bible. Say, for instance, the topic of work along with the book of Proverbs piques the interest of your people. You might develop a sermon series such as "Proverbs' Perspective on Work." Or, if the survey results reveal that your congregation is hungry for the topic of leadership and curious about the book of Exodus you could create a sermon or series called "Leadership Lessons from the Life of Moses." You get the idea. Asking the flock about their sermon needs can help you help them.

EXERCISES

1. Modify the sermon survey above to fit your ministry context. Feel free to delete and add some topics and doctrines.

2. Designate the date when you will distribute the sermon survey. Think through all the logistics involved in distributing and collecting the survey during the corporate worship gathering.

3. Recruit someone to tabulate the results of the survey and decide when you will need the results for your sermon planning retreat and your sermon planning team meeting. Give clear instructions to the survey tabulator concerning the data in which you are most interested.

36

SOLICITING
SERMON FEEDBACK

Preachers can experience significant growth by intentionally soliciting feedback concerning their preaching. This chapter will investigate numerous ways that preachers can receive honest feedback about the strengths and weaknesses of their sermons.

If you are going to ask for feedback, you need to be ready for an honest response. One time my wife and I asked a friend to tell us who our newborn child looked like. We thought the friend would point to one of us. Instead she responded, "He kind of looks like Vince." Vince was a moody and, to be honest, miserable teenager from our neighborhood. That was not the answer we were expecting! After that, we stopped asking for feedback concerning the looks of our newborn.

Pastors are notoriously sensitive about receiving feedback on our sermons, even when the feedback is glowing. Like one of our children, the sermon is a part of us, an extension of who we are; it comes from the deep places inside of us and has our DNA all over it. Therefore, it's not easy for us to receive feedback revealing that our offspring looks different to others than they do to us. Some preachers stop asking for feedback altogether.

The truth is, without constructive, honest, and specific feedback, preachers will not reach their full preaching potential. All preachers tend to hit a ceiling of limitation in terms of natural skill. In order to break through this ceiling, we need some other voices for guidance. For preachers who want to improve, who are thick-skinned enough to welcome constructive criticism and humble enough to receive commendation, consider the following avenues for sermon feedback.

CONGREGATIONAL FEEDBACK FORM

Every six months, place a congregational feedback form in the bulletin to solicit sermon feedback. These surveys should be anonymous in order to facilitate honesty. Keep the survey to no more than five to seven questions that can be answered within three minutes. The form should yield feedback that is informative, helpful, and easily tabulated. You might want to include the following questions in your congregational feedback form: What is the one thing you appreciate most about the sermons preached in this church? What one change would you recommend to improve the sermons preached in this church? What recent sermon had the most positive impact on your relationship with Christ? Why do you think that sermon had a positive impact upon you? What other feedback can you give us to improve the sermons preached in this church?

SERMON FOCUS GROUP

The sermon focus group allows preachers to solicit and receive more thorough feedback than the survey, but from fewer people. This group might consist of fifteen to twenty people who represent a cross-section of your congregation in terms of age, gender, ethnicity, and spiritual maturity. Select people who are able to insightfully analyze and constructively critique sermons. Invite this group to serve by meeting with you four consecutive weeks for an hour immediately following the worship service or before Wednesday of that week. Develop and distribute a discussion guide for the focus group. Perhaps the following questions can be included in the focus group guide: At one point in the sermon, did you most encounter God or become inspired? How did the Bible inform and guide the sermon? Did the sermon connect with your life situations? In one sentence, what do you think the sermon said overall? Do you feel the delivery of the sermon, in terms of the preacher's voice, body, and face, helped or hindered the content of the sermon? Solicit feedback from the month-long sermon focus group twice annually. Select a different group every year.

PREACHING COACH

The most specific and potentially helpful feedback you will receive comes from a preaching coach. This preaching coach can be a member of your congregation or a pastoral colleague from another church. If you choose the latter, perhaps you can coach each other. A helpful format is to meet with your preaching coach four to six times annually. You will want to meet in an office where the two of you can listen to one of your sermons. After the sermon, invite the coach to speak words of commendation and critique into your preaching life. Be careful not to get defensive or you will limit the feedback your coach wants to give you. Commit to listening and only speak when you need to ask questions for clarification on your coach's feedback.

Listening to your sermon with a preaching coach who is poised to critique you is extremely awkward, but get over it! A preaching coach can help you progress toward your preaching potential with long strides. If you recruit a coach from within your congregation, be sure the person is supportive and secure enough to tell you the truth about the strengths and weaknesses of your preaching. In order for you and your coach to have a common language for feedback, try utilizing a sermon feedback form like the one below so you don't enter the meeting with different expectations. You could also adapt some of the questions from the form to your congregational survey and focus group.

A SAMPLE SERMON FEEDBACK FORM

CONTENT
What did the sermon say about God and the gospel?

Theology: What did the sermon say about God—Father, Son, or Holy Spirit?

Gospel: Describe whether or not the sermon captured the essence of the gospel by dealing with both the problem of human sin and the grace of God.

Exposition: Could you see how the sermon flowed from the biblical text? Explain.

Structure: Explain whether or not the structure of the sermon had focus and flow.

Clarity: In one complete sentence, write the focus of the sermon:

On a scale of one (low) to ten (high) rate the *content* of the sermon:

CONNECTION
How well did the sermon connect with the context?

Images: Did any illustrations, stories, or metaphors from the sermon connect with you at a significant level? If so, which ones and how did they appeal to you?

Relevance: Did the sermon connect with the situations of your life in a relevant manner? If so, how?

Application: Did you come away from the sermon with a sense of why and how to live into the gospel reality it proclaimed? Explain.

Passion: Do you think the preacher spoke with passionate conviction? If so, why?

On a scale of one (low) to ten (high) rate the *connection* of the sermon:

CHARACTER
Was the preacher congruent with the Gospel?

Competence: Do you think the preacher was spiritually and mentally prepared for the preaching event? Why or why not?

Authenticity: Did the preacher communicate in a manner that was genuinely congruent with her or his personality? Explain.

Delivery: Did the preacher's eyes, body, and voice help or hinder your receptivity to the sermon? Explain.

Love: How did the preacher, through the sermon, evidence love for God and for people?

On a scale of one (low) to ten (high) rate the *character* of the sermon:

EXERCISES

1. Reflect on the times when you received feedback regarding your preaching. How did someone's commendation of your preaching encourage and empower you? How did someone's constructive critique help or hinder you?

2. Develop a detailed timeline for your sermon feedback plan. On what two Sundays this year will you distribute a scaled-down feeback form to your entire congregation? During which two

months of the year will the sermon focus group meet? Who will you invite to serve on the focus group? On which four to six days in the coming year will you meet with your preaching coach? Who would make a great preaching coach for you? Go ahead and put the names and dates on paper. Then, commit to your plan with rugged determination.

37

DEVELOPING A PREACHING GROWTH PLAN

The first time I played eighteen holes of golf my score was ninety-six, thanks to the help of a few mulligans. I was told by some veteran golfers that ninety-six is a very good score for beginners. Well, I have been playing golf off and on for approximately twenty years now. Just about every time I play, which is not too often, I score between ninety-six and 110. Although I had a decent start to my golf career, I have not improved at all in the twenty years I have been playing this frustrating game. I have actually gotten worse!

My golfing woes used to get the best of me. Why am I not getting better at the game? Why are some of my buddies improving and I'm not? I was ready to throw in my clubs until I realized a sobering truth. The reason for not improving was the lack of effort I applied toward getting better. If I was going to improve my game, there needed to be an intentional plan for growth. My friends improved by going to the driving range twice a week and playing a round once or twice weekly. They watched videos to work on their swing. Some of them even paid for a few lessons with a golf coach. The most serious among them actually read golf books and magazines, taking notes on what they read. Did they improve? Absolutely, but not without an investment of time, energy, and money.

I decided that if improving my golf game required the implementation of an intentional plan, then golf wasn't for me. But those who are called to preach the gospel of Jesus Christ cannot neglect our growth as preachers. If people are willing to develop a golf plan, career plan, financial plan, or exercise plan, how much more should the preacher be willing to develop a plan for growth? The following ideas can assist preachers who are ready and willing to develop an intentional growth plan.

READ DEEPLY AND BROADLY

One of the ways that preachers grow is by reading about preaching. There are many books you can purchase and free articles on the Internet you can access with a few clicks of the mouse. Consider reading an article on preaching every other day and a book on preaching every two months.

In addition to reading deeply on the subject of preaching, be sure to read broadly beyond preaching. There are several areas from which to read that can improve preachers and their preaching. Read about current events from publications like *Time* and *Newsweek*. Check out good biographies from your local library. Along with current events and biographies, read some classic and contemporary fiction. Reading fiction can heighten your preaching imagination (chapter 29). Finally, it is wise to read the number one best-selling book in America year to year, asking yourself the question, why is this book so appealing to people? This question may lead to fruitful insights for preaching today.

ATTEND SEMINARS, CONFERENCES, AND CLASSES

Pastoral ministry can keep us pretty busy and, at times, exhausted. Who can afford to spend time at a seminar, conference, or class focused on preaching? The real question for the preacher who wants to grow is, who can afford *not* to attend these growth-fostering events? While the number of conferences and seminars on preaching are in decline, the good ones are still going. Many Christian colleges and seminaries offer reduced rates for pastors who want to audit preaching courses. Stay fresh by taking the time to attend these skill-enhancing, soul-cultivating events. Make these events even more enjoyable and rewarding by inviting a few of your preaching friends to attend with you.

VIEW AND LISTEN TO SERMONS

Preachers who grow have a habit of insightfully observing the preaching of others and analyzing their own. An Internet search can lead you to audio or video of sermons from some of the best preachers today. I intentionally listen to an eclectic mix of preaching voices, in terms of age, gender, ethnicity, style, and denominational affiliation. I observe their preaching not to clone them, but to learn from the homiletic habits and convictions that surface in their sermons. I usually view these sermons when I'm running on my treadmill; this may be one of the reasons why I appreciate shorter sermons!

Another way preachers grow is by viewing their own sermons. This is rather uncomfortable for most preachers, but it is indispensible for growth. Get in the habit of listening to one of your sermons monthly and viewing one of your sermons every other month. Analyze the strengths and weaknesses of both your content and delivery. You may want to utilize the sermon feedback form in chapter 36.

SOLICIT FEEDBACK

In the previous chapter, we explored several ways to solicit evaluative feedback regarding our preaching. Congregational surveys, a focus group, and a preaching coach can help us discern both the strengths to maximize and the weaknesses to overcome in our preaching habits. If you sense a vital area for improvement emerging from this feedback, you can tailor your preaching growth plan specifically toward overcoming it.

EXPERIMENT WITH SERMON FORMS

Most preachers have two or three favorite forms we use to structure the sermon. Some may use the point by point propositional form with exposition, illustration, and application for each point. Others may gravitate toward a narrative form that structures the sermon with setting, problem, climax, and resolution. All preachers have their preferences but, as my wife advises when we're at one of our favorite restaurants, "Live on the wild side and try something you never tried before."

If you want to stay fresh in preaching, live on the wild side and experiment with new sermon forms. Try preaching a silent sermon, using only images to communicate. Try interspersing your sermonic words with songs and testimonies from people in order to reinforce your sermon's focus. Try a first-person sermon where you become one of the Bible characters in the main preaching text. Try preaching a sermon that holds back the point of the sermon until the last sentence you speak.

Mix it up and don't be afraid to try something you never tried before. You may discover that some of the new sermon forms you employ appeal to different learning styles represented within your congregation. Most of your people will appreciate your willingness to go out on a limb and experiment. Perhaps you can commit to trying one new, out-of-the-box sermon form every month.

PRACTICE SPIRITUAL DISCIPLINES

Practicing the presence of God through spiritual disciplines such as praying, fasting, Bible reading, giving, journaling, and confessing—to name just a few—have the potential to form holy, virtuous preachers. Good preachers tend to preach good sermons. The best preachers have something beyond homiletic skills and an endearing personality. They have the anointing of God's Holy Spirit upon them. These preachers not only talk about God, they walk with God, and it shows. Of course, preachers can try to fake spiritual anointing in various ways. The discerning listener, however, can sniff out an imposter. Communing with God through the practice of spiritual disciplines will make a decent preacher better and a good preacher great! What spiritual disciplines will you incorporate into your preaching growth plan to more intentionally invite the anointing of God's Spirit on your life and preaching?

EXERCISES

1. Incorporating each of the elements described above, sketch out a one-year, one-page preaching growth plan. Be as specific as you can. For instance, fill in the dates of the growth events you will attend, the titles of the books you will read throughout the year, and the spiritual disciplines you will practice.

2. Write a prayer to God that reflects your desire and commitment to grow as a preacher of the gospel. Express also your need for God's grace to form you into the preacher he has created you

to be. Pray this prayer as often as necessary throughout the year, particularly in the moments just before you preach.

3. Every year, draw up a new growth plan and write out a new prayer that reflects your most current needs as a preacher. Perhaps you will want to share your preaching growth plan with your church board to invite their support and accountability.

PART 5

POSTSCRIPT

38

TIPS FOR
BUILDING RAPPORT

In Aristotle's ground-breaking work on communication theory called *Rhetoric*, he observed that not only the *logos* (content) of the speech, but also the *ethos* (character) and *pathos* (empathy) of the speaker determine the audience's receptivity to the speech. Aristotle highlighted for speakers the importance of building rapport with the people to whom we speak. In a day when suspicions toward leaders run high, rapport between the preacher and listeners has never been more pivotal to the preaching event.

Whether you are the unfamiliar guest speaker at a community service event or the well-known pastor in a local church setting, there are a few practical ways you can build rapport with any group you address.

COMMEND THE CROWD

Parenting experts suggest that parents should be as quick to commend kids as to correct them. Commending our kids builds them up and opens them up to receive correction. The same is true for preachers when addressing a crowd. We should be as quick to commend as we are to challenge people with our message. If you are the guest speaker for an event, this is especially important. Let the people know you appreciate, for example, their hospitality, their work in the community, or their core values. If you are the pastor of a local church, find some good things to say about your congregation that relate to the message you are preaching. Remember to be honest, creative, and insightful when commending a crowd.

USE SELF-DEPRECATING HUMOR

One of the ironies of public speaking is that the less seriously we preachers take ourselves (within reason), the more seriously the congregation may take our message. The apostle Paul was quick to admit his weaknesses, even humorously criticizing his lack of eloquence and poor eyesight, in order that his message on the cross of Christ might have prominence. The people to whom we preach are measuring our level of egotism. If they sniff out pride in us, it will diminish their level of receptivity to the message we proclaim. Self-deprecating humor, done naturally, wisely, and sparingly, gives the impression that we preachers see ourselves not as one *above* the people but as one *among* the people of God. Be careful not to overdo it. There is a line that can be crossed using self-deprecating humor that will actually inhibit congregational receptivity to the message. Our use of humor should not come from a position of insecurity but from one of security in Christ.

BE BRUTALLY HONEST

While the gospel of Jesus Christ is good news, it is bad news first. Before people even reach out for Christ, they must face the bad news that we are sinful, broken, and needy and that life is often unfair, lonely, and empty. Unless a preacher speaks to the painful realities of life that humans experience and endure, the good-news hope that God sent his Son Jesus to redeem what was dead and to restore what was lost won't be received with as much impact. If our preaching tends to sugarcoat the angst and suffering of the human condition, most people will quit listening to our message. Of course, the preacher must be just as honest about the good news too, even when the realities of the human condition attempt to veil the hope of the gospel.

DEMONSTRATE PASSIONATE CONVICTION

Another essential way to build rapport with the people to whom we preach is to communicate as if we really believe we have something life-giving to say. As our intimate connection to Christ increases, the more that passionate love for people and God surfaces within us. Some preachers can fake passion; maybe they even write reminders on their sermon notes like "Scream loud now," "Pause and cry," or my favorite, "Strain your voice and whisper so people think you have passion." I confess there have been times when I went to preach and felt a lack of passionate conviction about the sermon I was about to deliver. Those sermons, as you may know, are hard to preach and perhaps shouldn't be preached. I have observed that when a sermon proclaims good news worth living and dying for, it naturally creates the passionate conviction that builds rapport between the preacher and congregation. Simply put, passion is stirred in the preacher when the sermon is intently aimed at the glory of God and the liberation of people.

SCRATCH THEIR ITCH

Harry Emerson Fosdick, pastor of New York City's famed Riverside Church, said, "No one comes to church to find out what happened to the Jebusites." Fosdick was humorously advising preachers to steer clear of our pet issues so that we address the deep questions that listeners are asking. Preachers are notorious for not scratching in places where people are itching. We commit this crime in two ways. First, we raise questions in the sermon introduction that people aren't asking. Our rapport is diminished as people start daydreaming about stuff that really matters to them, like what they'll eat for lunch. The second way the preacher commits this crime is by promising, usually in the sermon introduction, to scratch a significant human itch and then failing to allow the gospel to actually do the scratching. This second form of the crime is worse than the first because it leads to a greater sense of disappointment in listeners whose expectations are built up and then let down. So, let's make sure our sermon not only elicits, but also scratches a significant human itch.

EXERCISES

1. Which one of the rapport builders above come most naturally to you?

2. Which one of these tips is most challenging for you? Why?

3. What other tips for building rapport would you add to the list?

39

PREACHING ON
HARD TOPICS

There are several hard topics, such as sex, capital punishment, generosity, suffering, abortion, euthanasia, divorce, and war that a pastor will likely have to address at some point in the life of a congregation. Hard topics are hard for two reasons. The first challenge is overcoming the sensitivity and defensiveness that some topics evoke. Topics such as financial generosity and sexual purity are sensitive and put people on the defensive, because many people tend to personally struggle with one or both issues. At certain points during a sermon on one of these hard topics, there is pin-drop silence and a high level of discomfort. That cannot be totally avoided.

The second challenge is that the Bible may not address these hard topics directly or clearly. The Bible does not directly address issues like euthanasia, which means the preacher must hunt for texts that inform the topic indirectly. It doesn't happen often but there are times when Scripture appears to offer divergent perspectives on a given topic. The topic of war is an example. War is certainly covered in Scripture, but it is a challenge to discern the overall canonical voice concerning the topic. The Old Testament is full of war and, it appears, God's endorsement of war. Yet, a case for pacifism can be made by simply focusing on some texts in the New Testament such as Jesus' words: "All who draw the sword will die by the sword" (Matt. 26:52).

No matter what hard topic the preacher tackles, there are several practices that can decrease the defensiveness of listeners and increase the likelihood of the sermon being received.

CONNECT THROUGH HUMOR

If the preacher can get people laughing, defenses usually come down. Humor should come early in the sermon before getting into the nitty-gritty. However, the call for humor is not a license to be callous, shallow, or rude. Humor should be creative and on topic. Humor should not be employed merely for laughs but for strategic connection with the congregation (chapter 31).

PRESENT ALL SIDES

When preaching on a controversial topic, one on which there are many different opinions in the world or the church, try to accurately represent all sides. This is not to say the preacher must agree with every position or present every position as equally valid and viable. But if you want to bring people to a new way of thinking and living, they must sense that you at least understand their position and reasons for it. If you have represented the various positions fairly, people who take those positions are more likely to fairly consider the Bible's position on the topic.

FOCUS ON SCRIPTURE

This may seem too obvious to even mention, but all of us preachers can slip from the realm of what the Bible says and into the arena of what we think. Sometimes, what we think and what the Bible says may be incongruent. Listeners can often tell if a preacher is using the Bible to proof-text the preacher's opinions. Every sermon should evidence the preacher's wrestling with and submission to Scripture, but this is especially integral to the hard-topic sermon. In the same way that the preacher should fairly present various positions represented among listeners, the preacher should be sure, most of all, to fairly present the various voices within Scripture that inform the hard topic.

SPEND TIME PRAYING

Most preachers pause to pray at different points in the sermon preparation process, but the hard-topic sermon warrants more prayer than usual. Prayer allows the preacher to peek into the heart of God concerning the hard topic. Prayer also gives the preacher a love and empathy for people on all sides of a given topic. The practice of prayer aligns the preacher with the truth of God's Word and the grace of God's heart for all people. Time spent in prayer to prepare for preaching the hard topic is time well spent.

EXERCISES

1. What hard topic needs to be addressed in a sermon to help your congregation move forward in their relationship with Christ? Is each topic hard because it is not directly or clearly addressed in Scripture, because it is sensitive, or both?

2. As you reflect on each hard topic, consider the following questions: If there is a humorous side to this topic, what is it? What are the various positions that people in your church and community take concerning this topic? What Scripture passages directly address or indirectly inform this topic?

3. Pray for your congregation, community, and world concerning this topic.

40

DEALING
WITH SURPRISES

Audio-visual glitches, member outbursts, fainting bridesmaids, and light-fixture fires are just a few of the surprises that may surface during the sermon. My goal in this chapter is to simply highlight some of the surprises you might run into so that they are no longer surprises. Some of these unexpected and unwanted occurrences cannot be avoided, no matter how hard we try. Yet if we know what might happen during the preaching event, the shock is minimized and we can plan, in advance, how to respond in appropriate ways.

ANNOYANCES

Fire station alarms, police car sirens, crying babies, cell phones, pouring rain, talkative teenagers, intoxicated sleepers, and loud motorcycles are just a few of the annoyances I have endured during the preaching event. Some of these are unavoidable. Do your best to keep preaching over the noise in- and outside of the church. You will probably have to raise your voice a bit until the police car goes by or the baby stops crying. Address the problem of talkative teenagers with gentleness and tact, but not during your sermon. Remind people before the service to silence their cell phones. Remember that people are watching the sermon you live, perhaps more intently than listening to the sermon you speak. No matter what surprise surfaces, be sure to respond with grace and composure. When the time is right, address those annoyances you can alleviate.

OUTBURSTS

What do you do when a guy raises his hand in the middle of your sermon, and even though you manage to ignore him for ten minutes, refuses to put his hand down? Do you call on him or not? Well, I called on him, and my preaching momentum, it seemed to me, was lost.

On another occasion, a young man I will call the "preach it" guy showed up. I enjoy some verbal response to the sermon, but this guy was downright distracting. He sat in the second row and no matter what I said, every two or three minutes he would yell out with a screechy voice, "Preach it!" Many in the congregation were distracted and, along with me, on the verge of laughter for most of the sermon. It probably didn't help that the assistant pastor was sitting right behind the "preach it" guy, laughing his head off. There is nothing we can do about these outbursts. Developing a hospitable church culture that is welcome to all may even contribute to some of these outbursts. But it's worth it. Preachers must learn to ride out these outbursts without blowing our lids. Someday we may look back on these moments as fond preaching memories like I'm doing here.

AUDIO-VISUAL GLITCHES

In one of the churches I served, we experienced audio-visual glitches just about every week. Videos wouldn't play at all, or we would hear the sound without seeing the video or see the video without hearing the sound. This drove me crazy. When these videos were intended to be significant enhancers of my sermon, I was especially frustrated. If the video didn't play properly or the microphone would snap, crackle, and pop loudly, I would say something humorous to reduce embarrassment for our technical people, but inside I was fuming.

In order to avoid some of these glitches, find and train qualified people to run your church's audio-visual ministry. Make the financial investment in quality hardware and software. Until you acquire capable personnel and equipment, don't attempt to be overly clever or frequent with your use of technology. In my opinion, it's better to use plain old-fashioned words to paint the sermon's picture than audio-visual technology that may or may not work.

HEALTH PROBLEMS

Be prepared for someone in the wedding party to faint, an attendee to have a heart attack, or a kid to have an epileptic seizure. Most of us encounter these health scenarios at some point in our preaching tenure. It is very difficult to finish the sermon under these kinds of circumstances. Regardless of the severity of the situation and the size of the church, you will want to finish the sermon, perhaps with some modifications to the sermon's tone and length. You can prepare for these surprises by helping the church establish a detailed plan to respond to health crises. Also, when someone in the congregation becomes publically ill during the service, be sure to pause the sermon and lead the congregation in praying for this person.

BUILDING ISSUES

As I stepped up to preach the sermon, I noticed one of the light fixtures in the ceiling was on fire. Someone called the fire department, and I invited everyone to grab a folding chair and head outside for the sermon. The weather was great. With the fire truck in the background, I preached in the open air. It was fun. There are other building issues that don't have such a happy ending. When the air conditioner breaks in the heat of summer, you can expect people to fidget, fan, or fall asleep during the sermon. You want to keep the sermons shorter than usual until the air conditioner gets fixed.

Another building issue you may encounter is a power outage. This is the perfect time for a prayer meeting and the sacrament of Communion, both of which rely on spiritual, not electrical, power. The point is, be willing to adapt to whatever surprises that may surface during the service and be sure to demonstrate a high level of patience, grace, and calm.

EXERCISES

1. Recall some surprises you have encountered in life and ministry. What tends to be your knee-jerk response to surprises? How can you respond to future surprises with grace and assertiveness, resisting the temptation to be either passive or aggressive?

2. Reflect on which category of surprises above is most typical or likely in your ministry context. Develop a plan now to respond to those surprises when they surface again.

41

WEDDINGS
AND FUNERALS

The apostle Paul wrote, "Be wise in the way you act toward outsiders; make the most of every opportunity" (Col. 4:5). Sermons for special occasions are one of the ways we preachers "make the most of every opportunity" to proclaim good news to "outsiders." Weddings and funerals provide opportunities for the presiding minister to guide the couple and comfort the grieving. There is another reason why these occasions are worthy of the preacher's time and energy. Inevitably, non-Christian family members and friends of the couple or deceased will show up for such events. There will be people present who don't know or believe that Christ loves them. Some may never attend a church service, even though, deep inside, they are starving for good news and hope. As often as I can, I say yes to these special-occasion preaching opportunities. And, I pray and work harder than usual in developing these sermons that have the potential to reveal the power and love of Christ to those who have never experienced or embraced either.

While every wedding and funeral sermon is unique, due to the factors surrounding the marriage or death, there are a few general strategies that can maximize these special-occasion sermons.

SIMPLE BUT PROFOUND

The special-occasion sermon should be accessible to all kinds of people, since all kinds of people will likely be in attendance. A ten-point doctrinal treatise on the meaning of "original sin" will likely lose people. Simple does not mean simplistic or trite. Some of us have heard and maybe even preached funeral messages that overly simplified the pain and angst of death and grief. This is not what I mean by *simple*. Instead, I mean presenting a comprehensible message about marriage or death in light of the love and hope we find in Christ.

The simple message should be profound as well. Since most of the people in attendance will have been to numerous weddings and funerals over the course of their lives, I want what I say and how I say it to be creative, not typical. One way to do this is by using biblical texts that are not usually included during these special occasions and by pointing out realities of married life and the grief of death that are often unnoticed or ignored.

SHORT AND SWEET

Unless you are officiating the funeral of a long-time saint of the church, keep the special-occasion sermon short. *Short* means different things to different people, so we should probably investigate the parameters. A special-occasion sermon should, in most cases, last no more than fifteen minutes. The rationale for brevity is that many people in attendance will likely be unchurched and, therefore, not used to listening to a talking head without channel surfing. Fifteen minutes might even be a stretch for some. You want "outsiders," to use the apostle Paul's term, to hear your message, move closer to God, and consider attending the church you serve, or a church near where they live. Keep it short or they may never step foot in church again.

Keep it sweet too. By *sweet* I am not suggesting that you sugar-coat the challenges of marriage and death. Instead, I mean to make the message as appealing, interesting, and engaging as possible, without being so clever that you overshadow the couple, the deceased, or, worse, God. The special-occasion sermon is not the time to preach your favorite hellfire-and-brimstone-in-your-face kind of message. One of the premier goals of the special-occasion sermon is to not only guide the couple or comfort the grieving, but to move people in attendance at least one step closer to the God who made, knows, and loves them.

CHRISTIAN NOT CLINICAL

The special-occasion sermon should incarnate Christ. The love of Christ flowing into and through the couple is the necessary ingredient for a love-filled and lasting marriage. The hope found in Christ can do more for those experiencing the grief of death than hours of expensive therapy. When it comes to the special-occasion sermon, the preacher should present Christ not a therapy session. This is not to say that counseling has no value; indeed it does. Therapy can help married couples overcome obstacles and the grieving move beyond their grief. People can get therapy from a therapist, but from the preacher, they must get Christ. In our efforts to guide people in their marriage and grief recovery, we must present sermons that present Christ. Something happens to people when they encounter Christ through the words of the preacher. Let's not allow our special-occasion sermons to become a self-help speech instead of a proclamation of Christ.

Weddings and funerals provide rare opportunities for the pastor to address the deepest needs of the human race by proclaiming the good news of Jesus Christ. People who would never choose to attend a Christian service or who haven't attended in many years will show up for weddings and funerals that you officiate. When they do, you have a God-sized opportunity to share the "reason for the hope that you have" in Christ with "gentleness and respect" (1 Pet. 3:15).

EXERCISES

1. Develop a well of biblical texts from which to draw for special-occasion sermons. List five themes of a wedding homily that can address the couple getting married and proclaim the good news of Christ to those in attendance (for example, love, forgiveness, and commitment). Now, identify at least one biblical text that might align with and inform each of the wedding homily themes you listed.

2. List five themes of a funeral homily that can address the grief of a loved one's passing and proclaim the good news of Christ to those in attendance (for example, hope and heaven). Now, identify at least one biblical text that might align with and inform each of the funeral homily themes you listed.

42

FRESH INSIGHTS AND NEW PRACTICES

In the first section of this book, we explored the importance of Preaching and Preachers. The preacher's character and theological convictions about preaching are significant in the shaping of the preacher and the preaching event. Next, we considered the dynamics of People and Places in preaching. The congregational and community contexts are key factors that must inform the development and delivery of sermons for impact. The preacher who understands this will be more thoroughly equipped to speak into the lives of the people within these contexts. The Preparation and Presentation of the sermon, the focus of the third section, is where the person of the preacher and the preaching context culminate and intersect with the preaching task. Developing and delivering sermons that are faithful to God, the biblical text, and the preaching context is the ultimate goal of the Christian preacher. In the fourth section of the book, we considered the importance of Planning and Progress. Creating a thoughtful, contextual, and well-balanced preaching plan for your congregation is both necessary and valuable. Planning facilitates good sermons, while progress fosters good preachers.

Preachers who progressively get better with time take intentional steps to do so. The fifth and final section, Postscript, includes a miscellaneous sampling of dynamics in the preaching life that are secondary but significant enough to include in a book on preaching.

In the same way that a sermon aims at being applicable to the listener's life, it is hoped that this book will be applicable to your preaching ministry. Which sections or chapters are most applicable to your current preaching needs? Which sections or chapters reinforce your current practices? Which sections or chapters challenge your current practices? What changes will you make to your current practices based on your reading of *Preaching Essentials: A Practical Guide*?

As I expressed at the beginning, I pray that God will use this book to help us more fully discover or recover our God-given voice to preach the gospel of Jesus Christ in a way that transforms lives.

EXERCISES

1. List seven to ten fresh insights or new practices gleaned from this book that you will apply to your preaching ministry.

2. Take a DAWG (day alone with God) on a day you would normally work. Prayerfully process what you learned from this book about God, yourself, the church, and preaching. Spend some time praying for the Spirit of God to anoint you for the task of proclaiming the gospel in a way that sets captives free (Luke 4).

3. Have fun preaching and don't be afraid to try creative homiletic ideas, as long as they're faithful to the biblical text, the ministry context, and the God who called you to preach.

4. Remember that "He who began a good work in you will carry it on to completion until the day of Christ Jesus" (Phil. 1:6).